GETTING STARTED!

Some 1st Steps In Your Journey With Jesus!

Mary C. Brooks

Handmaiden4Him Publishing

COPYRIGHT PAGE
LIBRARY OF CONGRESS
CATALOGING-IN-PUBLICATION DATA

Copyright © 2013 CAROL BROOKS (Mary C. Brooks)

LCCN 2016915519

Paperback Edition ISBN # 978-0-692-77596-7

New Title: Getting Started! Some 1st Steps In Your Journey with Jesus!

Previous Title: *Especially For New Christians Revised Edition*

ALL RIGHTS RESERVED
INCLUDING ALL INTELLECTUAL PROPERTY RIGHTS!

No part of this publication may be reproduced, stored in a retrieval system, or transmitted, in any form, or by any means, for example: electronic, mechanical, photo copying, recording, audio or otherwise, or manually without the prior written permission of the author.

Summary: An initial discipleship book for the new and young Christian and some back to the basics for the mature Christian.

Scripture quotations are from the King James Version of *The Bible*.

1. Discipleship, New Christians.
2. Converts, New, Religious.
3. Christian Living.

DEDICATED TO MY SON

My prayer is that JESUS will always be very real to you, your wife, all the children and their families (for all generations to come) till Jesus comes again.

May each of you fulfill the plan, purpose and calling that God has for each of your lives. I pray all of you will always be very aware of God's love for you and walk daily with His presence manifested. I pray all of you will hear His voice clearly, obey it quickly and always be yielded to the leading of The Holy Spirit. I pray Jesus and the truth of God's Word will be seen in each of your lives. I pray that your love for God, Jesus, The Holy Spirit and God's Word will grow stronger with each new day.

May Jesus Christ be glorified in each of your lives. May all of you walk in the truth and wisdom of God's Word and in the joy of His presence; knowing that God will never leave nor forsake one who truly belongs to Him. In the Holy and Precious Name of our Lord and Savior Jesus Christ I pray these things, Amen.

With Much Love,

Mom

ACKNOWLEDGEMENTS

Wow! In giving "Acknowledgements," I'm not sure where to begin.

Obviously, the first one is to God, our Lord Jesus and The Holy Spirit, without Whom none of this would ever have been possible. How very grateful I am, and humbled, that God has allowed me the privilege of being His vessel as He ministers through this book to whomever.

For ALL those who have prayed for me, the book and the spiritual blessings that God will give to all who read or hear about the book, "Thank you!" Only Heaven will reveal the fruit and power of your prayers! You have been so diligent and faithful over the years. I am so grateful! Words cannot express how your prayers have helped keep me focused, encouraged, uplifted - and kept the awesomeness of God's provisions coming in. Once again, God, His Word and the power of Prayer, have prevailed!

To Joyce Standley who proofread the original book, to Sandra Comer who helped proof read this revised and expanded one, to Lynn Nations who took the book cover I designed and made it into a reality, "Thank you." For all those who laid hands on the book, prayed over it and claimed all kinds of Spiritual Blessings for those who read and hear about it, "Thank you!"

This has never been my project. God spoke to my heart many years ago and said that He wanted me to write a book that would help feed His lambs/children. Even as the years went by, God never allowed my faith to waiver in what He wanted. By His Grace, I obeyed what He said. Then, many years later, He told me to write a new and expanded version. He gave me the wisdom, knowledge and time to bring this book to where it is today. God also gave me a new name for the book: *GETTING STARTED! Some 1st Steps In Your Journey With Jesus!* May God Bless all who were there for me (in any way) through the writing of this book – in Jesus' Name, Amen

TABLE OF CONTENTS

CHAPTER   **PAGE**

Prayer of Gratitude

Foreword

1. Now That You're a Christian, Where to From Here?   1

2. What Can You Expect From God? What Does He Expect From You?   5

3. What is God's Calling and Purpose for Your Life?   25

4. Some Confirmations of Knowing God's Will For Your Life   37

5. How Do You Communicate With God and How Does He Communicate with You?   41

6. Characteristics of God's Voice   59

7. How Do You Seek the Face of God and Draw Near to Him?   61

8. What is the Unforgivable Sin?   81

9. What is Spiritual Warfare?   83

GETTING STARTED! Some 1st Steps In Your Journey With Jesus!

GETTING STARTED! Some 1ˢᵗ Steps In Your Journey With Jesus!

TABLE OF CONTENTS (Continued)

CHAPTER	PAGE
10. The Love of God	93
11. Learning to Trust God	101
12. Letting God Love You	107
13. Waiting on The Lord	115
14. What About Tithing?	119
15. Old Testament Names of God	125
16. Moving Forward Ways to Study *The Bible*	*129*
17. Which Version of *The Bible?*	133
18. Some Basic Helpful Tools	135
19. A Daily Quiet Time	139
20. Other Insights from Scripture	143
21. Warnings from Scripture	147
22. How to Pray for the Lost	155
23. Scriptures to Pray for the Lost	157
24. Talking About Salvation	165

GETTING STARTED! Some 1st Steps In Your Journey With Jesus!

MY PRAYER OF GRATITUDE

Heavenly Father, I praise You for allowing me the privilege of "Being the Pen of a Ready Writer" (Psalm 45:1) in whatever ministering You do through these pages.

By the power of Your Holy Spirit, I ask that You anoint this book and prepare the hearts of all who will read, hear or even know about it. Minister, I pray, to each person as only You can, that which You want to say to them, in Jesus' Name, Amen.

Heavenly Father, I ask that You bring each person to a saving knowledge of Jesus Christ. Send laborers quickly to disciple them, that they may grow in Jesus and be able to disciple others also.

I pray Jesus will be revealed to each of them in a more glorious way than they ever could have imagined. May they never tire of seeking Your face. May they look to You for absolutely everything they will ever need being assured that You who have begun a good work in them....will perform [finish] it (Philippians 1:6). I pray all these things in the Holy, Precious and Powerful Name of our Lord Jesus Christ, Amen.

GETTING STARTED! Some 1st Steps In Your Journey With Jesus!

FOREWORD

This book is intended to be a helpful tool (an initial rocket boost of-a-sort) as you, a "NEW" Christian begin your walk with our wonderful Lord Jesus Christ. *<u>It is, in no way, intended to be presented, or taken, as exhaustive</u>*! I believe God will speak (and make Himself known) to His children in absolutely any way we are willing to hear and see Him. Some people look for God in the smile of another person or in a kindness shown to them by another person. Some look for Him in a quiet time, scripture, prayer, music or a sermon. Still others look for Him (and revel in the Glory of His presence) during a time of praise and worship. My prayer is that you will seek God in every area and circumstance of your life. Make yourself available and say, "Speak Lord, Thy servant heareth" (1st Samuel 3:10).

Then, be obedient to whatever God says to you. He is not hiding from you, or any of His children. He greatly desires fellowship with you – with all of His children. God sent Jesus so that we could be restored to fellowship with Him.

GETTING STARTED! Some 1st Steps In Your Journey With Jesus!

LOOK FOR JESUS IN <u>ALL</u> THINGS!

For it's true:

> "In all things, our eyes will see
> that which our heart loves." [3]

<u>NOTE TO THE READERS</u>:

FOR EMPHASIS PURPOSES, I have, at times, underscored, put in quotes or capitalized a few things that I feel are especially important for you to note - as you read through this book.

I hope that helps.

The Author

- - - - - - -

Chapter One

NOW THAT YOU'RE A CHRISTIAN - WHERE TO FROM HERE?

Sooo, you've accepted Jesus as your Lord and Savior. You're on a spiritual high that you never knew existed, but you also have all these questions floating around in your head! You're excited, and at the same time, just a little uncertain about all that has happened to you. You want to tell absolutely everybody you meet about Jesus and what He has done in your life - and yet, you feel so inadequate.

Wow, isn't it great! Allow me to add to your Spiritual high by assuring you that, even though the road isn't always easy, God's Grace is always sufficient. Victory comes through keeping an open mind and heart before the Lord and, most of all, a teachable Spirit. Armed with those things and the Word of God, your enthusiasm for Jesus will only grow into something more beautiful than you could have ever imagined. Believe me,

LIFE WITH JESUS IS NEVER BORING!

One of my constant prayers is that God, by His Grace, will never allow me to lose that child-like wonder and amazement of Him. He is so perfect in all that He does! Falling in Love with Jesus is not something you do just once - it's a life-long process that gets sweeter and sweeter with each passing day and year – *and YOUR Journey - is just now beginning!* How exciting! You have so many things to look forward to as you get to know Jesus one-on-one.

There will be times when you walk gloriously in His Presence. Just as important, however, are the times when He allows you to go through the valley. But, take heart, Jesus has not left you – nor will He! He, through the power and presence of The Holy Spirit, will go ahead of you, walk the valley with you and even cover you from the rear (Isaiah 52:12; 58:8). God promises NEVER to leave you, nor forsake you (Hebrews 13:5). Perhaps others have disappointed you; however, God will not. He promises, in His Word, that nothing, or no one, can ever separate you from His Love (Romans 8:39). There is one thing, however, that God cannot and will not do. He cannot and will not, lie. If you see something in His Word (Scripture), you can bank on Heaven and Earth passing away; but His Word will not! God will always keep and honor His Word!

By the way, you might like to know that there are over 3,000 promises in *The Bible*. It's a good idea to pick up an inexpensive book that lists these promises (usually costs just a few dollars at your local Christian Book Store). READ AND STUDY THE PROMISES GOD HAS GIVEN HIS CHILREN. You would do well to start right now memorizing Scripture, even short verses. You will find that most, if not all, of God's promises contain conditions. For example, the first promise in Scripture is listed in Deuteronomy 5:16 and has a condition that goes with the promise. It says that if children honor their Father and Mother that their days will be prolonged and that it will go well with them. Does that surprise you? You are in for many surprises as you search the hidden riches of God's Word! Allow me to give you another example. Scripture says, "If You abide in Me and My Words abide in you, ask what you will and it shall be done unto you" (John 15:7). I feel very safe in saying that God wouldn't have any trouble getting any of His children to claim that promise - would He?

Ah, but look closely at the condition for receiving this wonderful, powerful promise. You must abide in Him and allow His Words to abide in you. You can have the promise - but only if you're willing to meet the condition!

Let me go the second mile on this topic. I want to mention just one other promise to you (and there are many, many more). This promise is just as important as the ones mentioned previously.

Scripture says "Confess your faults one to another (the condition) and Pray for one another (in this case, a second condition), that you may be healed" (God's Promise) (James 5:16). Did you lose just a little enthusiasm on that one?

Be encouraged my precious brother or sister. After you have walked with Jesus for a while and He's dealt with pride on your behalf, you'll see the day when you'll quickly confess your faults, (and just for the record, we ALL have them). But, you'll also learn that just as quickly as you confess them and ask God's forgiveness, He will forgive, heal and restore you.

Chapter Two

WHAT CAN YOU EXPECT FROM GOD? WHAT DOES GOD EXPECT FROM YOU?

The answers to these questions are, in reality, a lifetime full of answers; however, let me to share just a few with you. At this point, allow me insert the definition of a bond servant. In Old Testament times, when a slave had been set free, some would choose to stay with their master and serve them out of love. As an indication of this decision, the slave would take a small spike (called an awl), push it through his ear lobe and attach himself to the door of his master's house. This was a sign to the master (and the watching world) that, even though he had been set free, that he had made the decision stay and serve the master because of his love for his master. That's how it is with us and Jesus! No, He does not require us to respond in the same way that the Old Testament bond servant did. However, He has set us free from sin and Hell - and we do freely choose to serve Him – because we love Him! That, and a grateful heart for all Jesus accomplished through His death at Calvary and His Resurrection should always be our motive for serving The Lord Jesus.

Later, in John 15:15, Jesus said that He no longer calls us "servants" (because a servant knows not what his master does), but said that He now calls us "friends." That's because He has made known to us ALL the things that He has heard of God, His Father.

However, in one respect, our responsibility does remain the same as that of the Old Testament Bond Servant.

It's the servant's total responsibility to serve, please and be obedient to the master. It's the master's responsibility to provide absolutely everything that the servant needs (be that housing, food, clothing, etc.). God, in His Word, promises to do exactly that for His children. The Old Testament calls Him Jehovah-Jireh (God will Provide) (Genesis 22:14). He tells us in Scripture (Matthew 6:8), He (God) "knows" what we have need of even "before" we ask. Isaiah 65:24 tells us that "While we are yet praying, He (God) hears." How beautiful! How marvelous and wonderful is God's Love toward us!

We have already established that God will never leave nor forsake us, that He cannot lie and that no one, or nothing, can ever separate us from His love. Rejoice in that, child of God!

HERE ARE A FEW OTHER THINGS YOU CAN EXPECT FROM GOD:

1. EXPECT HIM TO GIVE YOU THE HOLY SPIRIT, THE COMFORTER (Luke 11:13).

The Holy Spirit is the Power pack to live the Christian life!

2. EXPECT GOD TO CONTINUE ALL THE DAYS OF YOUR LIFE TO CONFORM YOU TO THE IMAGE OF HIS SON JESUS (Romans 8:29).

He tells us to "not be conformed to this world, but to be transformed by the renewing of our minds" (Romans 12:2). This comes by studying and meditating on God's Word). Why? The answer comes from Scripture in Romans 12:2: "So we may prove what is that good, and acceptable, and perfect will of God."

God WILL teach you His ways and grow (mature) you spiritually. However, the rate at which you grow depends a lot on how quickly and how willing you are to be taught, and how often you seek the Face of God, etc. How fast you learn to be obedient to the promptings of The Holy Spirit is a big factor also. A pastor once told a group of us:

> FIRST GOD gives – REVELATION
> (Tells us what He wants us to do).
>
> SECOND – HE requires – OBEDIENCE
>
> THIRD –AFTER - our Obedience,
> GOD GIVES - UNDERSTANDING
> (Hall). ₇

3. EXPECT GOD TO LEAD YOU WITH THAT "STILL SMALL VOICE." (I Kings 19:12).
> Even though God and Jesus reside in Heaven, (as a new Christian) The Holy Spirit now lives in you also and you are now a part of the body of Christ.

4. EXPECT GOD TO PERFECT THAT WHICH CONCERNS YOU (Psalm 138:8). God intervenes on your behalf and Jesus and The Holy Spirit makes intercession on your behalf (Romans 8:26, 34 & Hebrews 7:25).

> God will lead, guide and direct you through The Scriptures (*The Bible)*, the authority figures in your life and by the Spiritual discernment that The Holy Spirit gives you. God will also use open and closed doors to lead you. An important side note here: One

type of door (be it Open or Closed) is just as important as the other one. So, if you have sincerely sought The Lord about something and the door is closed, please (for your own good) do NOT try to force that door open. God may have something better in mind for you; or perhaps, it's just not His timing. WAIT for His leading. God's way and God's timing are ALWAYS best!

Often God will confirm His leading through your pastor, parents, husband, wife or another Christian. Scripture says it this way:

"Trust in The Lord with all of your heart and
Lean not unto our own understanding;
in all your ways,
acknowledge Him [God]
and He will direct your paths"
(Proverbs 3:5-6).

5. EXPECT GOD TO BE YOUR PROVIDER, HEALER, COMFORTOR ETC. - IN ALL AREAS OF YOUR LIFE.

God, and His Word, is the answer in everything. That applies in the spiritual, emotional, financial and physical areas of your life. However, this is a two-way street (relationship) with God, Jesus and The Holy Spirit. It has to be pursued as such.

6. EXPECT GOD TO NEVER ALLOW MORE ON YOU THAN YOU CAN WITHSTAND.

He promises that (with every temptation), He WILL make a way of escape (I Cor. 10:13). Whether, or not, you choose to take the way of escape that God provides for you is up to you! God always allows you the freedom to choose. The choice to be obedient to the leading of The Holy Spirit is, and always will be, YOURS to make.

An important lesson here is that even though the decision is completely yours to make, you need to make it wisely and prayerfully! The other side of the coin is that since you are free to make the choice, you are, therefore, responsible for the consequences of that decision. Even if it's a hard choice (one you might not want to make or something that you might not want to do), you can still cry out to God to help you make the right decision. God will give you the guidance, strength and wisdom to do anything that He calls you to do – anything that is His perfect will for you. Just an FYI: The more quickly you decide to go the way that God has prepared for you, the more heartache, trials and tribulations you will avoid.

**GOD'S WAY IS ALWAYS
THE BEST ROAD
TO CHOOSE!**

7. EXPECT GOD TO CORRECT (CHASTISE) YOU WHEN YOU ARE OUT OF LINE IN SOME AREA OF YOUR LIFE:
Scripture says that the Lord chastens those whom He loves (Rev. 3:19). His purpose is NOT to punish you or make things hard for you. He corrects you because HE LOVES YOU! He knows you will be much stronger because of the discipline you receive especially when that discipline is coming through the hands of a loving Heavenly Father who wants only the best for you.

Relax! Right now, you may feel that you have to do it all by yourself; but you don't. Scripture says that it is God who causes the growth – and gives the increase [for all of us] (I Corinthians 3:6-7).

The truth is - even when you (by Faith) accepted Jesus as your Savior and Lord, it was God who had already taken the first step in drawing you to Himself by, and through, The Holy Spirit (John

6:44). The Holy Spirit was convicting you that you needed to be saved (to repent and turn away from your sin). Your part and response, was the first of many years of saying "Yes Lord."

By the way, I once heard a pastor say that the total vocabulary of a Christian should always be:

"Yes Lord!" (Hall). ₇

One of your first responsibilities, (after praying and talking with The Lord about it) is to seek out a local Bible-Believing, Spirit-Filled church. If you're in church like that now, stay there. The Holy Spirit will prompt/lead you to go to another Bible-Believing, Spirit-Filled Church if, and when, that will serve God's purpose in your life. That may, or may not, come at a later time. God will let you know if He wants you somewhere else.

GOD WILL FEED YOU –
WHERE
HE LEADS YOU!

Two definite signs that you are where God wants you to be (as far as a church home) are that you will have peace about being there and you will know that you are being spiritually fed by The Word of God (Hall) [7].

Let's turn our attention now to WHOSE RESPONSIBILITY IT IS - TO DO WHAT in this new relationship with God, Jesus and The Holy Spirit.

It's <u>YOUR</u> responsibility to ask The Lord where He wants you to serve. It's <u>GOD's</u> responsibility to lead you to that place of involvement. Please notice that I said "involvement." Nowhere in Scripture does God call anybody to just warm a pew or just observe from the sidelines! Even as a new Christian, there is something you can help with in the church.

It's <u>YOUR</u> responsibility to faithfully attend the church that God leads you to attend and join. It's also <u>YOUR</u> responsibility to be baptized (if you haven't been already). Let the pastor, or a church leader know that you need to be baptized. It's <u>GOD's</u> responsibility to feed you at that church and to open doors of opportunities and places for you to serve and be involved. You need to let those in the church know that you are available and willing to serve.

A note of caution here – please do not accept an offer of any ministry position or responsibility that is beyond that of a new Christian's knowledge and experience. Hopefully, the church would not allow that to be offered to you at this point in time.

Right now, you just need to focus on growing in your personal relationship with Jesus and in the knowledge of God and His Word.

It's <u>YOUR</u> responsibility to "Seek the face of the Lord" (Psalm 27:8) and His Ways. It's <u>GOD's</u> responsibility to make Himself known (and very real) to you. God is not playing hide and seek with His children. That is NOT who God is, nor is it how He does things! He promises that when we seek for Him with all of our heart, that we will find Him (Jeremiah 29:13). God is very excited about us getting to know Him. He is very willing to reveal Himself to us. *The Bible* tells us we are blessed when we hear God (Proverbs 8:34).

It's <u>GOD's</u> responsibility to put Peace in your heart about the direction in which He is leading you. It's <u>YOUR</u> responsibility and free will choice to hear, acknowledge and act on, God's leading.

It's <u>YOUR</u> responsibility to endeavor to keep a Pure Heart before God and all men. Scripture says: "As much as is possible, live at Peace with all men" [that includes women too, of course] (Romans 12:18). Those aren't my words, they're God's. He knows there are some people who will not let us live at Peace with them. However, that does NOT give us the right to not try. God promises in Scripture that "When our ways please God, that He will make even our enemies to be a peace with us" (Proverbs 16:7). God promises to keep in perfect peace he [or she] whose mind is stayed on Him because he [or she] is trusting in Him (Isaiah 26:3).

Two important aspects of being at peace within ourselves are:

1) Being willing to forgive whomever for whatever they did or said that was wrong and that hurt or disappointed you.

2) Being willing to ask forgiveness for your words, actions or attitudes when something you've said, or done, was hurtful or disappointing to someone else.

Whether, or not, the other person chooses to forgive you is their choice to make before God. They will have to answer to Him for their decision – just as you will.

However, once you've done all you can do to make things right (with The Lord and with the other person or people), and you've sincerely asked the other person (or people) to forgive you, then be at peace. You've done all you can for now. So, for now, let it go. Give God time to work with them, but definitely keep praying for them.

Just remember, that when everything is said and done, you, and you alone, are responsible for, and accountable to, GOD - for your every word, action, thought, attitude and deed. Each person is responsible for their own! You are NOT responsible for someone else's words, actions, attitudes, thoughts, deed, etc.; but you definitely are for yours! That's a good thing to remind yourself of every day.

There is a Scripture that says "Thou God seeth me" (Genesis 16:13a). That can be a wonderful promise (if you're doing things right and need God to intervene). However, it can also be a warning, or a reprimand, if you're doing something that you know you should not be doing (no matter what that might be).

YOUR PART is to simply make sure you are in line with God's Word. Make sure you are not holding a grudge, or harboring unforgiveness in your heart, toward anyone for any reason. An important part of keeping a pure heart before God is to repent quickly when the Holy Spirit convicts you that you're wrong (or walking in sin) in some area of your life. Take the time to immediately make it right as soon as you can. This is for your benefit, as well as the other person(s).

It's **YOUR** responsibility to quickly confess your sin (acknowledge and turn from it) and to ask

God's forgiveness (and anyone else's that the Holy Spirit brings to your mind).

It's then <u>GOD's</u> responsibility to forgive you, cleanse and purify your heart and restore you to that place of beautiful fellowship (oneness of Spirit) with Him. Scripture beautifully says: "The pure in Heart shall see God" (Matthew 5:8).

Wow! What a promise! There are many benefits to being a clean vessel for The Holy Spirit to flow through! By keeping a clean heart and conscience, you will enjoy a greater depth of fellowship with, and usage by, our Lord Jesus! Another important reason to keep a clean heart before The Lord is so that your prayers will not be hindered. The Bible says in Psalm 66:18 that if we regard "iniquity in our heart" that God will not hear us.

It's <u>YOUR</u> responsibility to "Ask, Seek and Knock" (Matthew 7:7). It's <u>GOD's</u> responsibility to see that you receive, find and that the door is opened unto you.

ANOTHER IMPORTANT THING that you need to know (and it was touched on earlier) is that GOD absolutely will never violate a person's free will (their right to choose). He will always leave the final choice up to each of us. That includes everything, i.e., the decision to accept what Jesus did on Calvary, repenting, asking Jesus to come into our heart and be our Savior and Lord and every other decision in our entire life.

God wants you to choose to allow Him to live through you and to guide and direct your steps every day. He wants you to do this out of love for His Son Jesus Christ, and gratitude for what Jesus did on Calvary to pay our sin debt (that horrendous debt that none of us could pay). God wants you to know that you can trust Him and that He loves you. He wants you to know that He is in control of all things (regardless of how things may appear to be at the moment). He wants you to know that even though everything may not always be good that He promises in His Word that He WILL work all things to good "to them who love God and are called according to His purpose" (Romans 8:28b).

If God were ever going to make mankind do anything, it would be to get saved (accept what Jesus did on the Cross and through His Resurrection and come to a saving knowledge of Christ Jesus). But God has always given each person the choice to accept that Truth, or not.

The Truth is God did not make you get saved, neither will He make you stop sinning (no matter what that sin might be). It may be the sin of lying, stealing, adultery, gluttony, rebellion, pride, or just not being willing to admit when you're wrong and ask forgiveness from Him or someone else.

There's also another sin you need to deal with - if you haven't already. That's the sin of not being willing to forgive yourself for whatever you may have thought, said, or done, in the past. If you have confessed it to God (with a truly repentant heart) and asked His forgiveness, then, as a Child of God, He has forgiven you! Be careful not (even innocently) to set yourself above God. If the King of the Universe can forgive you, who, then, are you not to forgive yourself? Think about it!

God says that He removes the sin and remembers them no more. May I encourage you to do the same? Even when the enemy tries to remind you of those sins and condemn you with them once again, simply refuse to go there. Remind him that you are now a forgiven Child of God and that God has removed your sins as far as the east is from the west (Psalm 103:12) and that He remembers them no more.

The difference now in reference to sin is that since you have accepted Jesus into your heart, you can never be comfortable in sin ever again. The Holy Spirit of God is now resident in you and He won't allow it. Part of His job is to convict you of sin and wrong. If you've done, or are doing, something wrong, you will know it. You will be a lot more sensitive in discerning when something is wrong than you were previously. You will not find peace within yourself until you turn away from whatever it is and have nothing at all to do with it.

That's simply how God operates and it's for your good! All that God does (past, present and future) is, and always will be, is for the good of His children. You may, or may not see and understand that at the time. Trust Jesus, He knows what's best for you! Listen to Him and be obedient to what He says. One thing to be very aware of is that whatever Jesus says to you through The Holy Spirit will always line up with God's Word, *The Bible.*

Be of good cheer my Christian brother or sister! The Holy Spirit is now available to empower you with the courage, determination and the ability to let go of all sin (and, with God's help, to turn from it forever.) You are no longer alone in the battle! There are at least three others are in the battle with you! Yes, three others: God, The Father, Jesus The Son, and God The Holy Spirit.

Jesus is sitting at the right hand of God making intercession for us (Romans 8:34). The Holy Spirit also "intercedes for us according to the will of God" (Romans 8:16).

<u>YOUR PART?</u> Simply be willing to be obedient to what God is telling you to do - one day at a time. Ask Jesus to help you walk gloriously in the victory that He has already bought for you when He died on Calvary and rose again on the third day.

God is very willing to show you how to walk in DAILY victory.

As you grow Spiritually, God may also teach you how to help others walk free in Christ; but first you have to learn how to apply Scripture to your own life.

Remember, if you have accepted JESUS as Savior and Lord and are still walking (or living) in sin – then you are a volunteer!

**JESUS BOUGHT YOU VICTORY OVER SIN!
YOU DO NOT HAVE TO CONTINUE
TO LIVE ANY LONGER THEREIN!**

Jesus stands very willing to fight any and all battles with, and for, you. The Holy Spirit will show you how to walk in God's strength, the power of God's Word and anointing of The Holy Spirit.

The Bible says in Nehemiah 8:10 that the "Joy" of the Lord is our strength. That's a great thing to remember and pray - that you will walk in the Joy of The Lord.

Sin no longer has any power, or place, in your life
– that "<u>you</u>" don't give it!
So, by the Grace of God, the Blood of Jesus
and the power of The Name of Jesus
refuse to give it any place in your life - at all!

Perhaps, right now would be a good time to take a minute and pray. A good prayer would be to ask The Holy Spirit of God to reveal to you whatever needs to be changed (in whatever area) in your life. Ask God to give you the Grace to walk obediently and in victory in whatever The Holy Spirit reveals to you. Then receive that victory in Jesus' Name.

Remember too that The Word of God says: "...if any two of you shall agree on Earth as touching anything that they ask for, it shall be done for them of My Father which is in Heaven" (Matthew 18:19). So, you might want to get a fellow Christian to pray with you about whatever.

Just a side note: The use of the word "agree" here has the implication of a blending [adhering together] as though the two are one – inseparable – on the issue.

If you don't already have a prayer partner (someone to pray with on a regular basis; or as prayer needs come up), ask God to send you someone for that purpose. It's better for a woman to be partnered with another woman and a man with another man as prayer partners. The main thing is to be careful not to open a door for any possible temptation(s) in any realm. That includes even the closeness of sharing prayer times together. Always err on the side of caution for the good of everybody.

God is so very happy that you have allowed Jesus into your life and your heart! That fact, alone, brings a BIG SMILE to His face because you (His child) are extremely important to Him!

The Bible **says in Zephaniah 3:17 "The Lord thy God....He will joy over YOU with singing."**

**GOD JOYS
OVER
HIS CHILDREN
WITH SINGING!**

HOW AWESOME IS THAT!

GETTING STARTED! Some 1st Steps In Your Journey With Jesus!

Chapter Three

WHAT IS GOD'S CALLING AND PURPOSE FOR YOUR LIFE?

That is a question that every Christian asks The Lord sooner or later. The answer is two-fold. The First Part is the same for all of God's children. The Word of God says that it's God's will for His children to be family with Him, to fellowship, worship, praise, adore and show forth HIS Glory (Isaiah 43:7)! It's also God's will for His Children to be conformed to the image of His Son Jesus Christ (Romans 8:29). A good question to ask yourself is: "Do others see Jesus in my actions, words and attitudes?" If the answer is yes; then praise God! If the answer is no, then ask God to forgive you and grant you the Grace to do better. Remember, you are an Ambassador for Christ now. You represent Him to a lost and dying world. A helpful suggestion is taken from the book *In His Steps* (Sheldon).[11] Basically, the book suggests that you take a minute (in whatever situation you find yourself) and ask the question, "What would JESUS do in this situation?" This will give you the correct response.

Part of God's will for every believer is to be a witness (Mark 16:15), that is, to share the Good News that Jesus Christ saves and redeems. You may have also heard it referred to as "The Great Commission." Sharing The Good News of the Gospel of Jesus Christ and Soul Winning are just two different ways of saying the same thing.

One important and very effective tool in Soul Winning is sharing (or telling) your personal testimony (what Jesus has done in your life and how you came to accept Him as Savior). The person you are talking with needs to know that, they too, can be forgiven of their sins and can be born again in their spirit to New Life in Christ. Tell them that this happens only through Christ's shed blood on Calvary, repenting of their sins, believing on The Lord Jesus Christ and asking Him to come into their heart and life.

That is an important reason why it would be good for you to take a few minutes and write out your personal testimony. No one has to see it but you, at this point, and it doesn't have to be very long or super Spiritual. Writing it out and dating when it happened (best you remember) will benefit you also.

By getting things clear in your mind, you will be able to share them more confidently with others, especially initially. If you don't remember the exact date that you accepted Jesus as Savior, that's okay. If you need to (for peace of mind sake or to settle it in your spirit), pray again the sinner's prayer and ask Jesus to be your Savior. This time write the date on your copy of your personal testimony. If you ever have any doubts again, simply refer back to what you wrote and when.

Say what needs to be said in your personal testimony to give God glory and credit for saving your soul, but, also keep it as brief as possible. This will allow time for any questions from whomever you are talking with about it.

Let me take some pressure off about soul winning (witnessing to others about Jesus). You (nor any of us) are responsible for getting another person saved. In fact we CANNOT get another person saved. Only God can!

It's actually a four person process. Jesus has already done His part. As He said in John 14:6b, "... no man [that includes women and children] comes to The Father but by Me". This was accomplished by the shedding of Jesus' Blood on Calvary and by His Resurrection on the third day. There's something else that Jesus did toward a person's salvation even while He was still here on Earth. He interceded in prayer for all future believers. In John 17:20, while praying to God, Jesus said, "Neither pray I for these alone (talking about the ones who were already

His), but for them, also, which shall believe on Me through their word" (the future believers).

God's part is to draw the person to Himself. The Holy Spirit convicts the person of their sin and shows them the path to repentance. The last part is up to the person with whom God and The Holy Spirit are dealing. That person has to make the decision to accept Jesus' Love Gift of Calvary for themselves. No one can do it for someone else. God did not design it to work that way. Needless to say, Jesus, God and The Holy Spirit are quite good at what they do! The Heavenly Father knows exactly how, and when, to draw a person to Himself. The Holy Spirit knows quite well the best way to get a person's attention.

But, the bottom line doesn't change. God will always leave the choice of whether, or not, to accept Jesus as Savior and Lord up to each one of us individually. That is His bottom line!

There are, however, some things that we can do to help try to influence their decision for Salvation.

1. <u>First</u>, we can ask God to help us to live Godly lives in front of the lost (actually we should be doing that all the time anyway).

2. <u>Second</u>, we can pray and ask God to

remove the blinders from their minds, hearts and eyes (II Corinthians 3:14, II Corinthians 4:4 and I John 2:11) and ask Him to put His law into their hearts and write them in their minds (Hebrews 10:16).

3. <u>Third</u>, we can also share our personal testimony with them, as The Lord gives us opportunity. We can also pray for that opportunity.

4. <u>Fourth</u>, we can purpose to simply accept them for who, and where, they are at this point in time (someone who is not yet saved, but precious in the sight of God). Revelation 12:11 says that "They overcame by the Blood of The Lamb [Jesus] and the word of their testimony." I heard someone say (a few years ago) at a Church Session presented by a group of Christian businessmen that "One definition of Soul-Winning is doing or saying anything that helps a person come (even one step closer) to accepting Jesus as Savior and Lord." I'm not sure who said that, but I think the statement has merit.

Sometimes people are only ready for the next step (just one step at a time), so you have to be sensitive to that. A simple, yet positive, attitude toward Soul Winning is to Pray and acknowledge to God your awareness that it's His will for you to share Jesus with others. Then relax. God knows exactly when you're ready to share Jesus with another person. He knows, too, when that other person is receptive to hearing it. God's timing is always perfect!

Interestingly enough, Jesus didn't talk with, minister to, or even heal, everyone with whom He came in contact. He looked to His Heavenly Father for instructions and then He obeyed those instructions. You, too, have to tune your ear to listen for God's still small voice and then obey.

Your part is to love people, plant Godly seeds in their life and water the seeds if you have opportunity. Definitely pray over the Godly seed that have been planted in someone life. Pray also for a crop failure of all bad seeds that may have been planted by the world or wrong influences.

The Word of God says that one plants the seed, another waters and it is God who gives the increase/harvest (I Corinthians 3:6-7). God will give the increase (Harvest) in His time. That time may be when you witness to that person, or it may be another day. That's <u>**GOD'S**</u> responsibility - not yours.

Your part is to just make sure you're faithful to the leading of The Holy Spirit when He prompts you. If The Holy Spirit leads you, go to Romans 10:9-10, 13 in *The Bible*. Read these verses to the person. Ask them if they want to Pray and receive Jesus into their hearts.

If they say "Yes", simply pray the sinner's prayer of repentance with them. Then tell them about Luke 15:7,10 which says that there is joy in Heaven when even one sinner gets saved. Tell them that they just gave all of Heaven a reason to rejoice!

If they say no, tell them thank you for allowing you the privilege of telling them about Jesus and that you will continue to pray for them. Remember to do that. Keep praying for them that God will reveal Jesus to them, as only He can.

In the meantime, continue to love them and accept them as people whom God dearly loves, but who do not yet know Him. Lord willing, one day soon they will come to know Jesus as Savior! Never give up praying for them.

One of the most important things that Scripture teaches God's children is that we need to obey the leading of The Holy Spirit. I Thessalonians 5:19 says to "Quench not The Spirit." The Word of God says "...Behold, to obey is better than

Sacrifice..." (I Samuel 15:22). Psalm 32:9 says, "Be ye not like the horse, or as the mule, which have no understanding and must be held with a bit or bridle..." May I offer a word of encouragement about having to learn obedience? You may be interested to know that in having to learn obedience, you are in excellent company!

The Bible says "Though He [Jesus] were a Son, yet learned He obedience through the things which He suffered" (Hebrews 5:8). Since God required Jesus to learn Obedience (while He was here on Earth), then surely God will require it of us also. God's desire is for us to willingly, cheerfully obey Him, trusting Him that He knows what's best for each of us at any given time.

The Second Part of God's will, purpose and calling for His Children is very individualized (and personal) for each one of us. It appears that no two answers come in exactly the same way.

Scripture tells us that David was out tending sheep. He was called in from the fields (at approximately 15 years of age). Per The Lord's instructions, he was anointed king. I Samuel 16:12b says "And The Lord said, Arise, anoint him: for this is he."

I Samuel 16:13b goes on to say "...and The Spirit of The Lord came upon David from that day forward..."

However, even though David had been anointed king by Samuel, he was sent back into the fields to continue tending sheep and await God's timing for him to actually be king. David became king over Judah first. Several years later, he reigned over both Israel and Judah (II Samuel 5:1-4). David reigned over both of them for thirty-three years.

By the way, I can't let this opportunity go by without showing you (from Scripture) that God is not so much interested in your outward appearance as He is with what's in your heart. It's what God finds in your heart that's very important to Him (I Samuel 16:7). In this passage Samuel is looking at the outward appearance of Eliab and felt that surely this must be the one God had chosen, but God was looking at the inward heart of David. In Acts 13:22 God says "...I have found David ... a man after mine own heart, which shall fulfill all My will."

David had to go through a season of preparation to get to what God had called him to do. David had to wait on God's timing before he actually saw and experienced the manifestation of God's calling and purpose for his life. We have to do the same.

When God tells you, or impresses in your spirit, His calling or purpose for your life (in whatever way He chooses to communicate that to you), it would be good to write it down. Let God know that you heard Him and are paying attention! If it's of God, you absolutely cannot be happy doing anything else. Even though you may try to backburner it (put it off or not think about it), it will not leave you. The Word of God says: "For the gifts and calling of God are without repentance" (Romans 11:29).

There is a season of preparation for what God calls each of us to do. Don't doubt, resent or even resist it. It's during that time of preparation that God will teach, train, equip and mature you for the task and purpose He has for your life. Please do not resist God's leading, even if you don't always understand where He's taking you. He will reveal it to you in His time.

God would do you an injustice if He allowed you to tackle a job, or come into a position, without first preparing you. He knows you need that season of preparation. But, even with the season of preparation, there is, and always will be, an element of still having to totally depend upon, trust in, and believe God for the success in anything you are doing. That will never change. God doesn't want it to change. He wants you to know that He's there for you and will walk the path with you, no matter where the path may lead.

You can rest in knowing that God's timing is absolutely perfect. He alone knows when the time is right for what He wants in your life. He will have everything and everybody ready - at exactly the same time. God is never late! However, all the squirming in the world won't get God to change His mind and make things happen sooner than He has them planned, even though you might want them to happen on the time table of your choosing.

He has the bigger picture in mind (for everybody concerned). So you might as well forget trying to have your own way. Don't waste your time and emotional energy. Ask God to give you the Grace to just be still. Trust in and wait for His timing. He knows what He's doing! You will be a lot more at Peace by simply accepting that fact.

Being still, does not, however, mean doing nothing. Set your mind to learn absolutely everything God wants to teach you during this season of preparation. You'll be the better for it and it will make the time seem to go faster. Keep your spiritual eyes and ears open always. Stay tuned to and sensitive to the leading of The Holy Spirit as to how God wants to use you and reveal things to you during this time. Ask The Holy Spirit to lead, guide and direct you daily in the way The Lord would have you go. Commit your time and each new day to The Lord.

Don't try to second-guess God as to what He's doing in your life. He knows what He's doing and why! He has a plan and a purpose. He does not waste anything!

Romans 8:28 says: "...all things work together for good to them that love God, to them who are the called according to His purpose." God will use this time to accomplish His purposes in, through and for you, though you may not be able to see it right away. Trust Him, He's God and He sees everything from beginning to the end – all at one glance. He knows how He will work this time to your good. He's refining the gold in you as He's conforming you to the image of His Son Jesus Christ. How relaxed you stay, during this time of preparation and growing in The Lord, depends on you.

Take one day at a time. That's all God gives us anyway. Trust Jesus for what each of your tomorrows will hold according to His plan and perfect will for you. Never forget - God loves you!

- - - - - - -

Chapter Four

SOME CONFIRMATIONS OF KNOWING GOD'S WILL FOR YOUR LIFE

1). **<u>THE BIBLE</u>**

It's God's Love Letter, Directions, Map and Information Packet for every one of His children to help each of us to know His will and live the Christian life. Read and study it daily.

2). **<u>BY SEEING IT ALREADY ADDRESSED IN GOD'S WORD</u>** (*The Bible*)

You don't have to wonder, or even ask, if something is God's will, or not, IF He has already addressed it (said so) in Scripture (*The Bible*).

For Example:

You don't have to wonder if it's okay for you to lie. God has already answered that in Scripture. The Word of God says in John 8:44 that the devil is a liar, the father of lies and that there is no truth in him. Scripture is very clear on where the source of lying comes from.

3). **<u>BY PRAYING AND SPENDING TIME FELLOWSHIPPING WITH GOD</u>**
Listen for what God is saying to you. Be quiet and still before The Lord. See what The Holy Spirit will say to you. Write it down. That way you will be able to praise God for when what He has said to you becomes a reality in your life.

4). **<u>BY GOING TO AUTHORITY FIGURES</u>**
(Parents, Pastor, husband or Whomever) in your life. Ask them to pray with and for you for God to reveal his will, calling and direction for your life.

Be willing to hear what God will say to you through them.

5). **<u>BY NOT TRYING TO RUSH GOD</u>**

I don't recall who said:

"To rush God is to find fault with Him," and it makes sense.

Be at Peace! God knows your heart and your heart's desire.

Trust God and His Heart.
Trust His Love for you.
Trust His being All-Knowing and All-Wise about everything!

There's much comfort and wisdom in remembering that God is absolutely worthy of being trusted!

6). **BY NOT NEGLECTING ATTENDING CHURCH AND GATHERING TOGETHER WITH OTHER CHRISTIANS - AT CHURCH** (Hebrews 10:25)
Be in church regularly, seeking and praising God and asking Him to speak to you.

7). **BY TRUSTING THAT GOD DESIRES FOR YOU TO KNOW HIS PERFECT**

<u>**WILL FOR YOUR LIFE**</u> – and that He will reveal it to you – when the time is right and when He knows you are ready to hear what He, through The Holy Spirit, will say to you.

Often God will give verbal confirmation through one or more Christians. However, their words will only serve to CONFIRM what you already know in your heart – what The Holy Spirit of God has already said to you.

PRAISE GOD FOR THE HOLY AND
WONDERFUL GOD THAT HE IS!

PRAISE HIM
THAT HE LOVES YOU!

BLESSED BE THE NAME
OF OUR HEAVENLY FATHER
AND OUR LORD JESUS!

- - - - - - -

Chapter Five

HOW DO YOU COMMUNICATE WITH GOD AND HOW DOES HE COMMUNICATE WITH YOU?

That is a question every Christian wants to know the answer to, especially when they are new in The Lord.

There are many factors that influence hearing from God, communicating with, and fellowshipping with, Him.

One of the most powerful and effective means of communicating with God is Prayer. It always has been and always will be!

Speaking of which, have you prayed (talked with God) today? Have you expressed your love and adoration to Him today? He loves to hear from you.

Have you brought your needs, concerns and prayer requests before Him today? If not, I would encourage you to take a minute and do that. It will make you feel so much better knowing that you have given the concerns of your heart to your Heavenly Father. God wants you to allow Him to carry your burdens and walk with you through ever situation.

I Peter 5:7 says it well, "Casting all your care upon Him; for He careth for you." Will God answer you when you pray? Will He be found of you? The Word of God in Jeremiah 29:13 says He will.

> "And ye shall seek Me, and find Me,
> when ye search for me
> with all your heart."

The two verses that precede that one are important also (as is all of Scripture). Jeremiah 29:11-12 says, "For I know the thoughts that I think toward you saith The Lord, thoughts of Peace, and not of evil, to give you an expected end. Then shall ye call upon Me , and ye shall go and pray unto Me, and I will hearken unto you."

So one of the first step in communicating with God is to seek Him with all of your heart.

Matthew 7:7-8 says it this way, "Ask and it shall be given you; seek and ye shall find; knock, and it shall be opened unto you. For everyone who asks, receives; and he [or she] that seeks, finds and to him [or her] that knocks, it shall be opened to them."

In Luke 11:9-10 it says the same thing but starts by Jesus saying "And I say unto you..."

So how do you pray? What do you say to God? How do you address Him?

First of all, relax. God knows that you are new in The Lord. He understands that you don't know everything yet. In fact, none of us will ever know everything this side of Heaven. It's okay. God's just very happy that you asked Jesus to be your Savior and Lord. That's the most important thing to Him!

Just as we get excited when a baby speaks their first word, or takes their first step; so God gets excited when we first start talking with Him in Prayer. He loves it!

It's not about what words you use, or how eloquently you speak, the length of your prayers or even if your grammar is correct. It's all about the sincerity of your heart and what's in your heart. That's what gets God's attention. God simply wants you to share what's on your heart with Him as you Pray. He loves when you do that!

There is a balance when you come before God in prayer. It's about attitude and humility. But, it's also about knowing who you are in Christ Jesus, knowing who God is as a Holy God (respect), as well as boldness before Him. The balance in this is in humbling yourself and coming as a little child (Matthew 18:2-4), as when you first came into the Kingdom of God. We are also to come boldly before the Throne of Grace that we may obtain Mercy and find Grace to help in time of need (Hebrews 4:16).

Don't be the least bit concerned about anything Child of God. The Holy Spirit and Jesus are there with you to help you as you take your first steps in prayer toward your Heavenly Father.

REMEMBER, you are coming into the presence of someone who dearly loves you! He will help you learn how to pray.

It's as simple as just telling The Lord about the things that are concerning you and asking for His help. Then being quiet and still and listening for anything He will say in reply. He may speak through His Word until you get use to listening for His voice

Perhaps it would help you get started if you think about someone who is kind, caring and easy to talk to – someone that you really enjoy. You can talk with them about most anything. Think about how comfortable you feel opening up to that person, because you know that they genuinely care about you and what's going on in your life.

Don't try to focus on seeing that person's face, but only on how you feel when you're talking with them. You probably feel completely at ease with them; because you know that they really want to hear what you have to say. They care about you and you know that.

The truth is, God loves you so much more than that person ever could! Focusing on that will help you feel more comfortable as you learn how to pray. The more you talk with God and Jesus the easier and easier it becomes.

God has lined out in Scripture how we are to come into His presence. There is a time and a place for everything as we seek God.

There is a time to thank Him "Enter His gates with thanksgiving..." (Psalm 100:4) and a time to praise Him "...and come into His courts with Praise" (Psalm 100:4) and a time to "...Bless His Name" (Psalm 100:4). There is a time for bringing your prayers, supplications and intercessions before Him (I Timothy 2:1). There's also a time to be still before Him "Be still and know that I am God..." (Psalm 46:10a).

However, God also understands the urgent prayers we sometimes pray (when the depth of the hurt or cry is so great or when there simply isn't enough time to pray anything else). So, we cry out to Him -

"JESUS, HELP ME"

or

"FATHER GOD, HELP ME!"

God understand those prayers and the urgency of them. I'm sure He has answered many of those for all of us at one time or the other. What's important to God is that you're reaching out to Him and that you know that He's there for you.

But, let's get back to looking at being quiet and still before The Lord (Psalm 46:10).

Being "quiet" (ceasing from talking, praying, etc.) is important. When you're quiet before Him. It's much easier for you to listen and hear what He wants to say.

However, being "still" before The Lord is something else entirely. Psalm 4:4 says, "Stand in awe and sin not; commune with your own heart upon your bed and be still..." Being still means you choose (by an act of your will) to bring ALL activities to a complete stop! That includes all thoughts, prayers, praises, speculations and wishes about things you trying to figure things out.

You make a conscious decision to put everything out of your thoughts for the moment and allow your mind, thoughts and emotions to come to a complete rest - before The Lord.

Basically, it's choosing to just sit and rest at the feet of Jesus with no agenda of your own. Then say to The Lord, as Samuel did, "...Speak; for Thy servant heareth" (I Samuel 3:10).

God speaks in a still, small voice. (I Kings 19:12b). Therefore, hearing it is definitely easier when you are still and quiet before Him (and in a frame of mind to just listen to what He wants to say to you).

Be encouraged new brother or sister in Christ, God is not going to tell you to seek Him, and then not be found of you. That is not how He works. He just wants you and He to spend some quality time together. Those quality times together are very precious to The Lord. They will become the same to you also, as you fall more and more in love with Jesus.

At first you may treasure those times alone with God simply because you realize that He only holds the answer to every question you will ever have.

As time goes by and God reveals more of who He is to you (and you get to know Him and His Word better) thoughts about those times will change. You will come to value those times alone with God because of who He is and how much you have grown to love Him and His Word. You will rejoice in knowing how totally, unconditionally, without any hesitations or reservations that He simply loves you. God's Love for you is precious. He sees you as very valuable.

No one (other than Jesus and The Holy Spirit) will ever love you as unconditionally as God does! With all of our faults, shortcoming, weaknesses and human ways, God still loves and accepts us simply for who we are, uniquely and wonderfully made by Him.

We were made for fellowship with Him and to fulfill His plan, purpose and calling for each of our lives.

When you think about it, it's easy to understand why it's so important to God that you spend time alone with Him. Just as you enjoy spending time alone (in the natural) with someone you love, so God loves spending time alone with you. He delights in you! It's as simple as that. Yet, it's also profound in that The God of the Universe wants to spend time alone with each of His children; but, He does!

The redemption of all of mankind back to God is what Jesus' death and resurrection was all about. Fellowship with each of us is, obviously, very important to our Heavenly Father. It should be to you too. Never take the privilege of spending time alone with God for granted. Truly, it is a privilege! It costs Jesus absolutely everything, including His very life.

So, how do you approach this Holy God to talk with Him? First of all, you need to remember that God IS God! He is Holy, Majesty, All-Powerful, All-Knowing, All-Seeing Creator, Ruler of Heaven and Earth (and so much more). He is in absolute control of everything! You should always show a proper reverence (respect) for Him and His position as God!

What about Jesus? Where is He now? Jesus is in Heaven where He ascended after His resurrection (Mark 16:19). He is sitting, in all His Glory, at the right hand of God. He is continually interceding for those who are His (Romans 8:34) and those who will become His as He did in John 17:20.

Second, you need to remember when talking with God that He welcomes your company! He looks forward to spending time with you His family (and those who will become His family). He is never too busy to talk with or listen to you. He's available to all of His children 24 hours a day, 7 days a week, and 365 days a year. The Word of God says that God shall "...neither slumber nor sleep" (Psalm 121:4b).

So, again, how do you approach this Holy God? The answer is simple. Just as you would comfortably sit down with that dear, close, cherished friend that you completely trust (as we mentioned previously), do the same with God. The only difference is for you to remember to show the proper respect and reverence for Him as God.

Just as you would speak very freely, openly, honestly, and transparently with a trusted friend; speak with God in the same way.

There's no need to hold anything back when you're talking with God. He already knows about everything anyway, but He wants to hear about it from you.

He wants to hear you acknowledge that you are totally dependent on Him for the answer(s) that you need. Acknowledging that to God is not for His benefit, but for yours! It helps you keep things in a right perspective in your life and thinking.

When a person starts thinking that they can do everything and make decisions without God, Jesus and The Holy Spirit is when they usually get into trouble. They end up needing His help more than ever and also His Grace and Mercy to fix whatever they've messed up.

Jesus said, "Come unto Me, all ye that labor and are heavy laden and I will give you rest" (Matthew 11:28). The Word of God also says: "...let your requests be made known unto God" (Philippians 4:6).

Another way to know the will of God is through Open and Closed Doors. Both are important. Pray and commit the situation to God. Tell Him that you do not see His direction clearly but that you greatly desire to be obedient to HIS will and only HIS will (and make sure you really mean what you are saying)!

Ask God to close ALL doors that are not His will for you in the situation and to make known to you the open door. You may feel a prompting in your spirit to be still (that's it not quite God's timing yet), or you may feel the Holy Spirit of God prompting you to step out in Faith trusting God that He will confirm the right direction for you. Sometimes, GOD is waiting on us. In fact, most times God is waiting on us to come in line with something He has told us to do.

IF God has told you the next step to take, that's light on your path. Many times, God waits for our obedience before giving us more light on our path.

Whatever you do, or don't do, make sure your heart and mind are open to being obedient to the leading of The Holy Spirit, regardless of which way He leads. Keep your Spiritual ears tuned to the voice of God and your Spiritual eyes open to seeing the hand of God move.

Praise Him for His wondrous Love for you and for revealing His direction in the situation. Ask God to bless your efforts if you're headed in the right direction and to stop them if you're headed in a wrong direction. Then, trust Him to do that.

God is faithful! He will honor the sincere prayer from your heart prayed in Jesus' Name.

If you have asked God to intervene, lead, guide and direct you and then you find a major roadblock in your path, please, please don't try to find a way around it.

REMEMBER YOUR PRAYER and what you asked God to do! Just Praise God for answering your prayer according to His perfect will for you and all concerned.

It's very necessary that you be willing to allow God the freedom (and the right) to say yes, or no, to whatever you're asking for or praying about.

The KEY to reaching out to God and hearing God answer you is none other than child-like Faith. You must be willing to trust God to give you the answer that He knows is best for you. Be assured that He has heard your request (unless you have unrepented of sin in your life). If that is the case, please take care of it right away. It's important that you do!

Be assured that God will answer you in His time, which is always perfect. However, you must be willing to accept what happens (or doesn't happen) next in the situation. That's the real test!

Seeking God for an answer is very serious business from God's viewpoint. It needs to be very serious business from your viewpoint also!

One of the best ways to hear from God is to PRAY before you start reading, studying and meditating on Scripture. Call upon The Holy Spirit and ask Him to enlighten your understanding as you read God's Word. Ask God to speak to you and to reveal Himself to you through His Word!

God wants you to know His Word because He knows its light and life and truth for you. He knows that you allowing Him to show you how to walk in the Truth of His Word will bring Spiritual success to your life. It will also cause a closer personal relationship between you and Him, because Scripture reveals God, Jesus and The Holy Spirit.

The Holy Spirit loves revealing the depths of Scripture to the Child of God. That's one of His jobs.

Good news! There is always more to learn about God, Jesus, The Holy Spirit, the ways of God and *The Bible*– always! That's true no matter how long you've walk with The Lord Jesus! It's one of the exciting things about being a Christian.

There are always new heights and depths to excel to because *The Bible* is alive. Another factor is that you are constantly at a different place in your walk with The Lord Jesus, as you grow and mature in your Faith.

The Jesus of *The Bible* is alive, The Holy Spirit of *The Bible* is alive and certainly God of *The Bible* is alive! They all eagerly wait to guide you on your Christian journey which is starting now. The Christian life (one totally sold out to Jesus) is definitely an adventure! Living for Jesus is never dull or boring! There are always more things to learn about Him, God, The Holy Spirit and The Scriptures. There will always be more things to learn as you learn to apply Scripture to your life.

Life with Jesus is a very Earthly beneficial and Heavenly rewarded life. You will love and appreciate your journey as a New Christian (even more) as you get to know the awesomeness of our Lord Jesus Christ. You will fall more and more in love with Jesus every day.

God's Word says Love never fails (I Corinthians 13:8). Jesus is all about God expressing His love (through Jesus) for all of mankind. Make a decision to spend time communicating with, and listening to, God.

This brings us to another very important subject and that's learning to live one day at a time. It's not the easiest way to live, but, by God's Grace, it can be done!

It's impossible to go back and re-live yesterday. Neither can you jump ahead and live tomorrow. That only leaves today.

Worrying about the past, present or future is not something God wants us to do. Think about it. In its simplest form, worrying is simply not trusting God. As humans, all of us find ourselves worrying at times (whether we mean to or not). But, when you do, repent, make things right as best as you can, and then allow The Holy Spirit to remind you of who God is in your life. Repent of worrying or trying to figure things out for yourself. Allow God to restore your Peace. He's good at that!

Just a reminder, God never promised to send in next month's provisions (money or whatever) today. What He did promise in Scripture is to "...supply all your need according to His riches in Glory by Christ Jesus" (Philippians 4:19).

TRUST JESUS – HE IS FAITHFUL!

One more comment about obeying God today. I do not recall where I heard it, but someone said, "Do you realize that as you are obedient to God today, then all of your tomorrows are covered! You can't live next week till it gets here. By then, it's today anyway." So deal with it when it gets here. Trust God that His Provisions will be sufficient then also.

There is one thing you need to understand and see clearly from God's point of view. Actually you need to learn very early in your Christian walk to see everything from God's point of view. You need to understand that God sometimes has to say "no," or "not now" but, when He does, it's for your good! God is always interested in the good of His children.

If you ask for something that God knows will hurt you now or later, (be that physical, financial, spiritual, or otherwise), He has to say "No!" God knows what character qualities He's building into your life, what He's teaching you and also when and how He's teaching you. It could be you're asking for something would actually harm you or someone that you love. Perhaps it wouldn't have that same effect if He allows you to have it at a later date. But, trust Him; God knows what's best in the current situation and the future ones also. God says "...no good thing will He withhold from them that walk uprightly" (Psalm 84:11). God is committed to your good and to transforming you into the image of His Son Jesus Christ. He is gentle, kind, loving and merciful, but He can also be tough when He needs to be. The main thing you need to know is that He still loves you, even in the midst of the tough love times. His every thought and action is motivated by what's best for you and all of His children.

Child of God, it just can't be said enough – "You are dearly loved by God!" That doesn't mean you can get away with garbage in your life. He loves you too much to allow that, but you are His Delight and He keeps you as "...the Apple of His Eye" (Psalm 17:8).

God wants you to succeed in whatever He calls you to do, but mainly in your relationship with Him, Jesus, The Holy Spirit and God's Word.

He will provide everything you need for that success if you seek Him, His Word and obey Him as He leads you. God will walk every road with you. As a Child of God, you are never alone. He will never leave nor forsake you (Hebrews 13:5).

As mentioned, the absolute Number One thing that God wants you to succeed in is your personal relationship with His Son Jesus Christ. That's the place of greatest Blessing for you (and the greatest Joy to God), because it makes the cost of Jesus coming to Earth, dying on the cross and being resurrected worthwhile.

God also gives The Holy Spirit to guide and comfort you and to walk along side of you in every aspect of your life. That's one of the privileges of being God's Child! It's through the power and presence of The Holy Spirit that you know Jesus, have the truths of Scriptures revealed to you and have fellowship with God. The Holy Spirit is the living Jesus in the world today. God sent Him when Jesus ascended back into Heaven, so that we would have a comforter (John 14:16-18).

The Word of God in Philippians. 1:6 says, "Being confident of this very thing that He which hath begun a good work in you will perform it until the day of Jesus Christ." This is a promise from God.

Therefore, walk daily in the power of God's Word, and in The Name and Blood of our Lord and Savior Jesus Christ.

Be all that God has called (or will call) you to be for His Glory - in Jesus' Name.

"...BECAUSE GREATER IS HE
THAT IS IN YOU,

than he that is in the world"
(I John 4:4b).

Chapter Six

SOME CHARACTERISTICS OF GOD'S VOICE

This entire section on "Some of the Characteristics of God's Voice" comes from a 1981 cassette recording of a sermon by Reverend Peter Lord.

Per him - GOD'S VOICE is:

1. QUIET
2. PERSONAL
3. PRACTICAL
4. SIMPLE
5. DOWN TO EARTH
6. IT LEADS – IT DOES NOT DRIVE

Reverend Lord goes on to say that "A person who doesn't know how to hear God in solitude will never hear Him in the noise."

Reverend Lord recommends: "If you're not sure God said something - Ask Him." Then, give "Expression to the Impression."

He also recommends a Quiet time. Reverend Lord describes A Quiet Time as "A time when you deliberately tune out everything else and set your channel on God - not so much to talk to Him, - but to let Him talk to you."

**PRAISE THE NAME
OF THE LORD!**

- - - - - - - -

Used by Permission.

Chapter Seven

HOW TO SEEK THE FACE OF THE LORD AND DRAW NEAR TO HIM

God IS a Holy God. However, it's very important for you to realize that from the very moment you accepted Jesus Christ as your Savior, God no longer sees you as a sinner.

He now sees you as Holy and Righteous because He sees you through the Blood of His Son Jesus Christ. This is not because you could attain to that (because none of us can). It's because of what JESUS did on Calvary by the giving of His own life and His blood to pay for our sins. Once you have sincerely repented of your sins, asked God to forgive you of them, have accepted Jesus as your Savior and believed that God has raised Him from the dead, your Salvation is complete in Christ Jesus.

Once you have done that, *The Bible* says God remembers your sin no more and He removed your sin "...as far as the East is from the West..." (Psalm 103:12). You may already know that, because, as a New Christian, you have already come by the way of The Cross of Jesus Christ.

The Scripture does, however, say to "believe and be baptized." (Mark 16:16). The Word of God says "All who call upon The Name of The Lord shall be saved." (Acts 2:21). You are now a part of the Body of Christ. The Word of God says in II Corinthians 5:17, "Therefore if any man [or woman] be in Christ, he [or she] is a new creature: old things are passed away; behold ALL things are become new."

That will never change Child of God! God sees you as a completed work; even though, in reality, at this very moment, you are still a work-in-progress (as are we all). One important point to make here is that even when you mess up, God still loves you and welcomes you into His presence; no matter what you've done. He wants you to come to Him, repent and ask Him to forgive you and let Him make it is right again.

Don't run from God when you mess up, or fall short; but instead, run very quickly - to Him! That's where you help is – with God!

God says in Isaiah 43:21 that He formed us for Himself, that we should show forth HIS praise.

Seeking the Face of God and drawing near unto Him brings us back to coming into His Gates with Thanksgiving and entering into His Court with Praise (Psalm 100:4), because that's where it all needs to start. But, how do you do that? Here are a couple of things that should help you:

There are times when we must offer to God the "Sacrifice of Praise" (Hebrews 13:15); simply because there are times when (for whatever reason) we do not feel like (or feel worthy of) Praising the Lord. However, when we obey God, and do what His Word says anyway, it's amazing how easy it becomes!

IF you have difficulty coming into God's Presence with an attitude of thanksgiving and praise, you might want to start by just Praising Him for who He is - God Almighty, King of Kings, Lord of Lords, Ever-Faithful, and Never-Changing. Praise Jesus also for Who He is and that He is ever interceding before the throne of God for those who are His! That is so important, since Jesus intercedes for us when satan tries to accuse us before The Father!

You will get more familiar with each role of each of the three persons of The Trinity as you grow in God's Word.

Next, you might want to just thank God for many other things! Regardless of where you are in life, or what's going on in your life, you still have much for which to be thankful. Each one of us does! Gratefulness is a very important character quality for a believer to have, as is a spirit of appreciation.

Thank God for even the everyday things, such as waking you up this morning, letting you live another day, for your health, for saving your soul, for Jesus! Thank God for your job if you have one (or for the one He is going to give you if you don't currently have one). Thank God for His provisions (food to eat, clothes to wear and a place to live). Thank God for your family (both your natural family - and your Christian family). No family member is perfect, but then neither are you (nor any of the rest of us). We are all at various stages of being conformed to the image of Christ.

Thank God He is still working with all of us, to bring all of us to where we need to be in Christ Jesus. Thank God for Christian brothers and sisters who will pray for you and be there to encourage you along the way. Thank God for a Pastor who loves Jesus and is committed to teaching the Truth of God's Word and to lifting up The Name of Jesus. Thank God that your pastor is allowing The Holy Spirit to reign in the church that you are attending.

There are many things for which to be thankful and grateful. You need only to stop and think about them.

Once you have allowed The Holy Spirit to bring you into this spiritual frame of mind, Praise (and sometimes tears also), will flow freely as your heart melts before the awesomeness of our Heavenly Father and our Lord Jesus Christ.

One BIG thing for which you can be thankful - is that since you have repented of your sins and ask Jesus to come into your heart, He is now walking with you daily (through the power of The Holy Spirit). The Holy Spirit, the angels of Heaven, etc. are now fighting your battles either for, or with, you. You are now under the Intercessory Prayer covering of Jesus Himself and "...greater is He that is in you; than he that is in the world" I John 4:4.

Another important part of drawing near to God is that of repenting of any known sin in your life. Ask God to help you keep your heart, mind, will and emotions free from sin or anything that hinders The Holy Spirit from flowing freely through you. Ask God to protect you from anything that isn't in line with God's Word and His will for your life. DAILY seek to be a clean vessel through which The Holy Spirit can flow.

It's all about a heart attitude. The more you yield yourself, your thoughts, actions and attitudes to God, the faster you will find yourself dealing with, and repenting of, any sin that The Holy Spirit brings to your attention.

You may say, "But I repented of my sins when I accepted Jesus as my Lord and Savior." That certainly should be true! However, because none of us are perfect yet, it's necessary that when we do sin - to acknowledge that sin before God and ask His forgiveness.

It's also very important to understand that this, in no way, affects your Salvation. Your Salvation is secure in Jesus once you have sincerely confessed with your mouth The Lord Jesus Christ and believed in your heart that God raised Jesus from the dead.

Scripture says in Romans 10:9-10 "That If thou shalt confess with thy mouth The Lord Jesus, and shalt believe in thine heart that God hath raised Him from the dead, thou shalt be saved. For with the heart man believeth unto righteousness; and with the mouth confession is made unto Salvation."

> Jesus said in John 10:28:
> "...neither shall any man pluck them out of My Father's Hand."

What yielding to sin does, however, is affect your fellowship with God and The Lord Jesus Christ. Once you truly belong to God and Jesus, relationship with them cannot be broken. You are a Child of God and, even when we are faithless, God is faithful (I Corinthians 1:9). However, allowing sin to continue is not a good thing. Sin separates us from God until we confess it and ask forgiveness for it. So repent quickly and often. It's for your good!

Think about a time when you had an unresolved conflict, problem or difference with a friend or family member. Think of how that unresolved conflict hindered your fellowship (oneness of spirit) with them. The two of you were still family or friends, but both of you felt the wall (or walls) that were there. Those walls kept you from fellowshipping and being in harmony with one another.

That's how it is when we have unrepented of sin in our lives. It hinders our oneness of spirit (our fellowship) with God and Jesus. You would be wise to take a minute, right now, (there's no time like the present while it's on your mind). Make a commitment to yourself, that by an act of your will (and with God's help), you will not allow sin of any kind to hinder your fellowship and oneness with The Lord.

Just as soon as The Holy Spirit reveals anything in your life that is not pleasing in the sight of God (anything at all), do your best (with God's help) to clear it up as quickly as possible. That is being wise!

Proverbs 18:24 tells us that Jesus is "The Friend that sticketh closer than a brother." In I John 1:9 we are assured that "If we confess our sins,

He is faithful to forgive our sins and cleanse us from all unrighteousness." The beautiful part is that you don't have to do anything alone. God will show you the way out – the way to walking in victory in whatever, if you ask.

A clean heart and pure conscience before God (and people) is very critical to coming into the "Fullness of Joy" – that is found only in the Presence of God. Psalm 16:11 reminds us that "In Thy Presence Lord is Fullness of Joy." Do you want Joy? It's found in the Presence of God - fellowshipping with and Praising Him.

The Word of God also tells us that "...The Joy of The Lord is our strength" (Nehemiah 8:10).

An excellent suggestion comes from the book *Faith Is Not a Feeling* (Campus Crusade for Christ). In the book, they suggest learning to deal with things one brick at a time, thus not allowing a wall to go up between you and God (or you and others). Please remember:

**BEING TEMPTED IS NOT SIN,
HOWEVER - YIELDING TO IT IS!**

As a Child of God, you do not have to sin! Jesus, through His shed blood and resurrection bought us everything we need to walk in victory over sin.

As Children of God, we are without excuse. There is no temptation, but such as is common to man (I Corinthians 10:13a). There will be temptations in this world. Anticipate, watch for, and be on your guard for any temptations that the enemy might try to throw at you. Ask The Holy Spirit to keep you sensitive to any temptations and to give you the Grace to flee (run from) whatever that temptation might be. As a Child of God, you do not have to yield to the temptation. God absolutely will help you IF you ask Him. Be very quick to obey whatever The Holy Spirit says to you by getting away from temptation. If you are a child of God and you are in sin – you are a volunteer! You do not have to be there, nor do you have to stay there. It's your choice!

But, how do you get out of what you know is wrong? Pray, Repent, ask God's help and His Forgiveness. Forgive any others involved. Ask God to restore you to that place of "Whiter than Snow" (Isaiah 1:18). Ask Him to give you freedom of spirit again. Somewhere along the way I heard the quote "Repenting is simply acknowledging to God what He already knows is true" and, by His Grace, and with His Help, turning from it – and turning to God - and the way of The Word.

Another important thing to realize is that sometimes you may even be mad at God. What, mad at a Holy God? Yes – maybe - sometimes - if you're not careful. Does that surprise you?

Think about it. Who has the power to change the situation? God does! Granted, there are times when we can do some things to resolve the problem or make the situation better. We should do those things if we can (based on what the situation calls for and what's in line with God's Word). Maybe others can do something to make things better also. Everybody should do what they can to resolve the situation in a Godly way according to what God is doing in the lives of all people involved.

Be encouraged my Christian brother or sister, God understands your frustration about the situation. He knows, loves and accepts you right where you are (right in the middle of not understanding or not knowing the best Biblical response to the situation). He is willing to help you understand and know what to do, when you, in humility, come before Him, and ask Him.

An important lesson here is that you (or any of us) cannot come to God demanding our way, or demanding an explanation from God. He does not owe anybody an explanation, though many times, in His Mercy, He will give one.

Most probably, God is already working behind the scenes in the situation that you're concerned about, even though your natural eyes may not yet have seen the results of what He's doing!

A smart move is to admit to God that you have not totally trusted Him in the situation (IF that is the case). You can also pray these words from Mark 9:24b, "...Lord, I believe; help Thou my unbelief". Ask God to forgive you for not trusting Him to work all things to good according to Romans 8:28.

Pray against any roots of bitterness or resentment caused by hurts. Pray, always for the Lord to keep your heart pure and tender before Him. Pray for you to have God's kind of Love for all people - in all circumstances and all situations. Only God can grant that to you!

Remember please:

FORGIVENESS IS NEVER AN OPTION FOR A CHILD OF GOD!

God says in Matthew 6:15 that if we don't forgive others, then He will not forgive us. So, don't be stubborn and nurse a grudge. It is not in your best interest, or that of anybody else. From a sincere heart, ask God to forgive you for not being willing to forgive Him (or anyone else). Go and make it right with God (and that other person) as best as you can.

You need to be aware, up-front, that there are some people who are not willing to allow things to be made right between you and them (for now anyway).

However, as long as you do your part, the rest is in God's hands. It's up to HIM to deal with the other person or people, after you've done all you can to make it right.

God will handle it, in His time. He knows their heart and the perfect way to deal with them. Just make sure that your heart is right toward the other person (or people). If not, ask God to help you quickly change that.

You don't want hurt, bitterness, resentment, (and definitely not hatred) etc. in your heart, mind or emotions. The Word of God says, in I John 3:15, that "Whoever hateth his brother is a murderer..."

I believe it's a Chinese proverb (not sure) which says "Hate FIRST consumes the vessel - in which it is contained."

Make the right choice! Choose, by an act of your will, to forgive whomever. Let go of any hurts and hard feelings you may have toward them. Remember God's promise, "...Vengeance is Mine; I will repay, saith The Lord" (Romans 12:19).

Please take a minute and talk with God about whatever, or whomever, has hurt or disappointed you, even if that person is yourself. Make a decision right now, with God's help, to get things cleared up between you and them as soon as you can. If you don't, you will miss out on walking in Peace about the situation and/or the person.

By the length of this section, you can tell that I'm very familiar with repenting, keeping a pure and clean heart before The Lord, as well as, a clear conscience. That's important for all of us to do regularly.

That's also necessary to do as you "Seek the Face of God and Draw Near unto Him."

Another part of seeking the face of God and drawing near unto Him is something that I'm also very familiar with – and that is being in the presence of, fellowshipping with, and delighting in the awesomeness of God The Father, Jesus His Son and The Holy Spirit as they manifest their presence. God says to all His children, "And ye shall Seek Me and find Me when you seek for Me with all your heart" (Jeremiah 29:13).

There are no words to describe the sheer JOY of fellowshipping with God, Jesus and The Holy Spirit. They absolutely love spending time with all of God's children.

Once you have known and have become aware of the presence of God manifested, you will never be the same, because you have experienced first-hand the presence of God Almighty, The

Creator and Master of the Universe Himself manifested.

Fellowship with us (His Family) is ultimately WHY God created mankind and why He sent Jesus to redeem us back to a place of being able to fellowship with Him.

As a part of The Body of Christ we are family for God! What a privilege that is - to be counted as a part of the Family of God!

A Side Note to help you understand something: God loves us very much. satan hates God. If you recall satan wanted to be equal with God, which is why he (satan) got thrown out of Heaven. satan tries so hard to hurt God by trying to get us away from God, hinder us, or cause us to fall. But, it's not really about us at all.

It's all about satan's hatred for God and trying to do anything that he thinks might hurt God. The good news for us is that satan knows he can do nothing to stop God's plans for us and he can do nothing to us that doesn't have to go through God's hands first. satan knows, too, that his days are numbered until he (and all of his angels) will be cast into the Lake of Fire (Revelation 20:10 and Matthew 25:41). he wants to take as many people as possible with him into The Lake of Fire. Praise God, with Jesus as our Lord and Savior, none of us will be in there with him.

Getting back to the subject of this chapter - if you have followed through with repenting, asking forgiveness of your sins and gaining a clear conscience before The Lord, that's great! Then your heart, spirit and mind should now be in a wonderful state for doing exactly what we started out to do - and that's "Seeking the Face of God and Drawing Near to Him."

Your spirit should be now free from all the garbage and you should now be ready to worship God, for who He is and "...In the beauty of His Holiness..." (Psalm 96:9).

He's Lord God Almighty, Ruler of this universe, Lord of your life, your Healer, Provider, Friend, Protector, your all in all, and absolutely everything you will ever need! The Word of God says: "Give unto The Lord the glory due unto His Name..." (Psalm 96:8).

It's fellowshipping with and drawing near to God that allows you to experience the breathless awe of being in His Presence - the Presence of a Holy God, overflowing with just Pure Majesty and Holiness and abundant Love for you!

A word of caution - Never seek the experience of being in the presence of God. That would be wrong and you would miss out on such a blessing by doing that! Seek God, Jesus and The Holy Spirit for themselves! You will not be disappointed.

Just like you would seek to get to know someone you love, or someone you would just like to get to know better, seek to get to KNOW God, Jesus and The Holy Spirit in the same way! There are great Blessings are in getting to know each one of them.

How can I do that you may ask? Good question! The answer is in reading, studying and even memorizing *The Bible* (God's love letter to you). Another part of that is simply coming aside daily from the cares of life and spending time just sitting at the feet of Jesus, listening and talking with Him and God.

Learn to bask in the Love of God and Jesus. Singing songs to them (songs of their choosing - as The Holy Spirit leads) is a wonderful thing to do! It makes for special times between you and them.

Sometimes The Holy Spirit makes known to me a Hebrew song or music that I think might have been the type that Jesus would have listened to (and was blessed by) when He walked on Earth. I can just envision Jesus listening to, and maybe even getting caught up in, worship and praise to His Heavenly Father through the music. Maybe Jesus even sang along with the songs/music as we sometimes like to do today (Scripture does say in Genesis 9:6 that God made us in His image). We do know that God sings. (Zephaniah 3:17) says "...He will joy over thee with singing." I believe that Jesus does also, since He and God The Father are one (John 17:11).

Many Hebrew songs/music lift up praises to Elohim, Adonai, Emmanuel, El Shaddai, El Elyon, Jehovah and many of the other Names for God. Jesus would have loved that.

Praise songs like these of adoration for God would have blessed and ministered to Jesus because they were used to worship and exalt His Heavenly Father, whom He loved, and still loves, so dearly.

The Word of God says God made us in His own image (Genesis 1:27). Once you fall in love with Jesus, one of your joys and sheer delights is enjoying the fellowship of God and Jesus (through the power of The Holy Spirit) as you sing, play or just speak praises and songs of worship to both God and Jesus!

There are few things that are more humbling and uplifting, both at the same time, than a powerful Praise and Worship time before God Almighty and Jesus, The Lord of Heaven and Earth!

It's during these times of songs and music being offered up to them (as a token of love just for their pleasure and enjoyment) that it makes such a difference. These are times of just Blessing Them! It's not about me at all. I come away very humbled, and so blessed, just to have had the privilege of facilitating songs and music that make Them happy!

And, yes, I do know that they are the God Head and can manifest anything They want to hear, far greater than I ever could. However, I'm grateful that They allow me the Blessing of giving back to them in this way anyway. The Word of God says that God looks on the heart (I Samuel 16:7b). They know my heart. They know that I love them. That, too, is a Gift from Them (James 1:17).

Think about how it touches the heart of someone you love just to have them know that whatever you are doing, or saying, is purely for them and out of your desire to demonstrate your love to them.

Saying things like "This song is for You Jesus!" blesses me so much; because I know that it blesses Him (and God)! I know it brings a big Smile to Their face. What more could you ask!

If The Lord leads you, try it! It doesn't have to be a Hebrew song. Pray and ask God or Jesus what type of praise and worship music They would like for you to bring/offer to Him. Just offer the song/music to The Lord as a token of your love - from your heart to His. Do it for no other reason than just to bring joy to Him. He will honor that because it's from your heart - and He sees that! It doesn't matter if you can sing or not.

Don't forget to daily tell God and Jesus that you love Them! In Genesis 1:27 it says that we are created "in HIS image" and just as we like to hear someone tell us that they love us, God, Jesus and The Holy Spirit likes to hear us tell Them that we love Them too!

Praise, worship, adore and just love God our Heavenly Father and Jesus our Lord and Savior- not for what they can do for you – but just for who each of them are – and that they are truly worthy of our praise!

Colossians 1:16 tells us that "...all things were created by Him, and for Him." God loves for us to worship and adore Him. He will always bless the beauty of that worship back to us. I come away from those times of fellowship blessed on so many levels (and by God's Grace you will also).

Bottom Line – You come away having loved God – and having been loved by God. There's a warmth and love that is found during those times (of just you and God), that simply cannot be found anywhere else.

God, through The Holy Spirit, will refresh, refill and renew you. A word of caution my Christian sister or brother! God is very real, as are Jesus and The Holy Spirit. Please make sure it's the PERSONS of God, Jesus and the Holy Spirit that you are seeking - and not just some experience.

GETTING STARTED! Some 1st Steps In Your Journey With Jesus!

Why seek the gift,

When you can have
THE GIVERS?

- - - - - - - -

Chapter Eight

WHAT IS THE UNFORGIVABLE SIN?
(also called the Unpardonable Sin)

The ANSWER – in a nutshell is
"Blasphemy against The Holy Spirit."

Per Webster's Dictionary
on line - Blasphemy is:

"To speak of, or address with irreverence; to profane; the act of insulting, showing contempt for, lack of reverence for."

Jesus said that all sins shall be forgiven the sons of men...but, he [or she] that blasphemes against The Holy Ghost will never be forgiven and are in danger of eternal damnation (Mark 3:28-30). Jesus wanted us to know that blaspheme against The Holy Spirit is serious business and should be taken as such. That was not said to scare you, but to simply make you aware of the danger according to Scripture.

The Scribes and Pharisees were saying that Jesus "...hath an unclean spirit." Jesus answered them in Mark 3:30.

Jesus said that He cast them out "...by The Spirit of God..." (Matthew 12:28).

They said the Miracles He was performing (healing the people and casting out of demons, etc.) were of the devil.

That's when He warned that blaspheme against The Holy Ghost (Spirit) would never be forgiven (Mark 3:22-30).

Read again Webster's definition of blasphemy for more clarity. Ask God, in Jesus' Name, for His wisdom and discernment about this. He will give it.

Chapter Nine

WHAT IS SPIRITUAL WARFARE?
HOW DO YOU HANDLE IT?

What is Spiritual Warfare? Spiritual warfare is the battle that goes on DAILY – in the "Spiritual" realm/world between God's forces of good and the devil's forces of evil.

God, Jesus and The Holy Spirit (along with all the angels of Heaven) have either already won the battles by defeating the enemy(s); or they are fighting the battles for, with, or alongside every Child of God every day.

Actually, for the child of God, the battle is always The Lord's! He's with us, to help us, and to fight our battles for us. (I Samuel 17:47b and II Chronicles 32:8).

Jesus' shed blood at Calvary and His Resurrection defeated satan over 2,000 years ago. The devil also knows, that not only was he defeated by Jesus; but he is destined to be cast into the lake of fire and brimstone to be tormented day and night forever and ever (Revelation 20:10).

Because the devil knows his time is short, he's trying to wreak as much havoc as possible and take as many people as possible to Hell with him. However, as always, all of mankind has a choice as to where they will spend eternity.

Every person does have a choice! Through Jesus Christ no one has to allow the devil to have any part in their life now, in the future and certainly not in eternity.

God is the devil's real enemy - and his greatest fear! That is why the devil tries to come against us, because we are God's Children and he knows that God loves us.

However, God is an excellent parent! He looks after His own! There is no way the devil can get to the Child of God without first going through God, Jesus and The Holy Spirit; unless we, usually though some sin our lives, give the devil some place of intro into our lives. So be diligent not to give, or allow the devil any place in your life (or that of your family).

He is always looking for a place to get a foothold in the life of the believer. So, don't allow it! You, as a believer and follower of Christ Jesus have power and control over that. So please make sure you don't open any door to let the enemy try to influence you or affect your life, your family's life or your witness for Jesus!

Say a resounding "NO!" to any way the devil tries to get you to do, or say, wrong things, think wrong thoughts, treat people in wrong ways, go down wrong paths or compromise on the truth of God's Word! Cry out to God for help if you need it! He will lead you in the right direction.

Sometimes the right direction is to get things that are not of God out of your house, off of your computer, off of your cell phone, IPad, Tablet or any other electronic device (be that at home, at work or in your car). ALWAYS PRAY FIRST, ALWAYS, and ask The Holy Spirit to guide you about this, what you need to get rid of or not.

Maintaining family harmony is very important. Remember that before the first thing is removed, or thrown away, it must be your right to get rid of it. It must be done with the right spirit, humbleness and much prayer. It must be done with love and respect for each other and each other's property. Love always reign (I Peter 4:8).

Keep in mind that the goal here is to cleanse your house of any "thing" that would give the devil even the smallest foothold in your or your family's life.

If you are not the authority figure in the household (or these items do not personally belong to you), they need to be dealt with differently.

If the item, or items, do not belong to you, and you are not the authority figure in the house, then the decision to remove them, or not, is not yours to make.

Please love and respect the other person/people enough to confront them about getting rid of these items. Please be sure to let them know that you only want God's best for them. Talk with them in a spirit of truth, gentleness, humbleness and love.

Pray and ask God to help them understand where you're coming from on this. Ask Him to help them see that you are only trying to protect them both in the Spiritual and natural realms.

Examples of some of these items are:
- Sexual magazines.
- Anything pornographic in nature whether in your house, on your computer, or on anything electronic including your cell phone.
- Anything that represents other gods.
- Books that portray wrong morals as being okay.
- Any kind/type of music that you (or someone else in your home) is listening to that you know is not pleasing in God's sight, regardless of what type/kind of music that may be. This music can be on:

Records, tapes, CDs, DVDs or maybe they were downloads to your cell phone, computer or other electronic devices. Head sets and ear phones take music, words, etc. directly into your head (without distractions). This means you need to be very careful what you listen to when using these or similar devices.

- Be sensitive to the music on the radio also. Turn off anything that is un-Godly in nature. That's for your good and anyone else that is hearing it.
- Violent video games are another thing that are of concern (mainly for the sake of your children). Some children spend many hours a day, or week, in front of a video, game screen or television). It may help Mom and act momentarily as a baby sitter while she does other things; but, in the long run, it's the kids who pay the price for the time spent interacting with these types of programs.

Ask The Holy Spirit to show you which items need to go, and then determine the best way to destroy them. The main thing is to get them out of your house. No, don't give them to someone else to take into their home. You definitely would not be doing them a favor if you did that.

If The Holy Spirit is telling you to get rid of an item and you're trying to justify keeping it, you need to pray and ask God why you're fighting against getting rid of it. Ask God why. Deal with whatever He says to you. Then by the power of The Holy Spirit, and through the shed blood of Jesus, and in The Name of The Lord Jesus, speak to the situation and break the hold (or any power of influence) that the enemy is trying to have over you, or anyone else in your household, through whatever it is, (no matter what it is).

Pray and ask God to replace where that thing, or things, were with His presence and with the Peace of God in your home. Pray the blood of Jesus over and a hedge of protection around your home.

So often, in Scripture, God (or His Angels) tells the children of God to FEAR NOT!

For the child of God, there is no need to fear, unless you're being rebellious, willful, and stubborn or are living in direct violation of God's Word or His directive to you. At times like that, you need to have a reverential fear of a Holy God who loves His child, but will discipline him or her for their own good.

That's very different from the type of fear that the enemy tries to bring upon you and tries to get you to buy into. You need to simply remember that God does have ALL things under control, regardless of what anything may look like and the lies that the enemy may be trying to get you to believe.

You will learn other things about Spiritual Warfare as you grow in the Lord. However, as a "New" Christian, you might want to focus on the following to start. This is simple, yet very powerful (because it's the Word of God)!

Read Ephesians 6:10-18. It tells you how to "...Put on the whole armor of God..." Be sure to get into the habit of doing this DAILY. Early morning is a very good time for you to do this.

In James 4:7 Scripture also tells us to:

1. "SUBMIT yourselves to GOD."
2. "RESIST the devil."
3. "AND he WILL FLEE from you."

the devil does NOT have a choice in this. Once you have done what God's Word has told you to do, he has to leave. This is a very simple, but powerful thing to do. Learn to apply it to your everyday life as needed.

One very important thing is that you make sure that you do not have any unconfessed sin in your life that is allowing the devil some sort of foothold in your life or the lives of those in your household.

I know of no place in Scripture where it says for us to fight the devil. The devil is a defeated foe. **JESUS HAS ALREADY DEFEATED** him! That is forever settled in Heaven and Earth! The Word of God does say, however, (as mentioned above) for you to submit yourself to God – then "resist" the devil. Matthew 16:19 and 18:18 both say that whatsoever we "bind" on Earth shall be bound in Heaven and whatsoever we loose on Earth will be loosed in Heaven.

So binding satan and/or the powers of darkness, evil influences, etc. is in line with God's Word. One note, it's extremely important that when you bind any evil thing and it's powers here on Earth, that you also loose the opposite good thing in its place, For example: Replace peace, integrity, harmony, love, kindness, forgiveness, the spirit of cooperation, etc. for the spirits of confusion, unforgiveness, disharmony, lust, etc. Do ALL in The Name and through The Blood of The Lord Jesus Christ.

This is God's Word and our authority to act on it as believers in Christ Jesus comes by, and through, the Blood of Jesus at Calvary and in the Name of our Lord Jesus Christ.

Again, you do not need to fight the devil – he has already been defeated! It's a done deal, and just for the record:

JESUS ALWAYS WINS!

Dr. Charles Stanley (Senior Pastor of First Baptist Church Atlanta, GA) says, "Fight ALL of your battles on your knees in Prayer and you'll win every time." [12]

If you are not physically able to kneel, God understands; so don't feel bad or be concerned (at all) if there is some physical reason you can't kneel to pray. Just rejoice over the fact that God hears the prayers of His people - regardless of their posture.

The truth is: You can talk to all of the people you want to about something, and you may see some measure of change. However, it's not until you bring whatever it is to JESUS, and talk with HIM about it, that things really get changed.

But be prepared, child of God, even when you bring things to Jesus, you have to be willing to wait for Him to answer - in His timing. God alone knows what's best! Praying to God is where the victory comes; so the sooner you commit it to Him, the sooner your answer will come!

I heard a story about a college student who was supposed to write a paper on God and the devil. The story goes that the student wrote and wrote about God. Time ran out and in very small letters – at the bottom of the last page the student wrote: "Didn't have time for the devil."

That's a great example for us to follow - putting all of our attention on God - and allowing no time for the devil.

- - - - - - -

Chapter Ten

THE LOVE OF GOD

If you are not a Christian and have not yet accepted Jesus as Savior, you simply cannot know and experience the Love of God in the way that God wants you to know and experience it. You have to know Him first!

Having a head knowledge of God (and knowing a lot of facts about Him) is definitely not the same thing as knowing Him personally. The same is true of Jesus and The Holy Spirit.

For example: I could hear and read many things about you from a variety of sources. Truth is, I could learn lots of information and facts about you, but it's not until I meet you personally, and spent some time with you one-on-one in some way that I would really get to know you. That's the same way you get to know Jesus, God and The Holy Spirit.

Interestingly, The Word of God (*The Bible*) says that when you get to know Jesus, we see God also. Even though each of them has different personalities and very different roles, God and Jesus are one. The Holy Spirit also is a part of the Three in One. Jesus said "I and My Father are One"

(John 10:30). He also said: "...he [or she] that has seen Me hath seen The Father..." (John 14:9). In John 6:46 Jesus said, "Not that any man [or woman] hath seen The Father, save (except) he [or she] which is of God, he [or she] hath seen The Father."

Before He left this world and returned to Heaven, Jesus prayed for all who were true believers at that time. But, not wanting us to be left out, He also prayed for all those who would become believers in Him in the future. Jesus covered ALL Christians in His prayer (John 17:9b, 20). So you were prayed for by Jesus even before you were born. How truly awesome is that!

John 17:11b records what Jesus praying to God said: "...Holy Father keep through Thine own Name those whom Thou [God] hath given Me that they may be One as We are." In John 17:22 Jesus prayed "And the Glory which Thou gavest Me I have given them that they may be One even as We are One."

But Jesus did not pray for those who would choose to walk the way of the world. He said "...I pray not for the world... (John 17:9).

So who is our fellowship with anyway? I John 1:3 says "...and truly our fellowship is with The Father, and with His son Jesus Christ."

Each person of The Trinity (God The Father, Jesus His Son and The Holy Spirit) has their own unique and distinct personality and function in The Trinity.

Let's look closer at each person of The Trinity, while keeping in mind the title of this chapter is:

"The LOVE of God."

<u>GOD THE FATHER</u>: If you're a parent, you may understand more readily, (from the parent perspective), the tremendous amount of LOVE that it must have required of God to allow His only Son, Jesus, to die in our place for our sins. He not only sent Jesus to Earth to die for our sins, but also to literally go to Hell and back for our sins - sins that Jesus did not commit.

God sent Jesus to die for ALL of mankind (that included the people who rejected Him as Messiah and Savior back in Bible times and also the ones who reject Him as such today).

To say it another way, God allowed His Son, Jesus, to be the sacrificial lamb for the sins of everybody in the entire world, both believers and non-believers. It was a packaged deal and paved the way for every human being to have a way (if they choose to take it) to come back into fellowship with God. However, God will not force any person to accept His gift of Redemption through Jesus. He will not violate man's free will.

Which of your children would you be willing to let die in the place of other people? In addition, some of the people may be very vile and wicked, who wanted nothing to do with you or your child. Could you still send your child to die in their place? God did.

Could you, as a parent, stand by and watch your child be beaten, spit upon, mocked, lied about, and finally having his hands and feet nailed with spikes to a cross? God did, while all the time knowing that Jesus was completely innocent of ALL the charges against Him. Only by God's Mercy did this happen, that and Jesus' love for God, and His obedience to the will of God and His love for us.

God's LOVE for us (you, me and the rest of the world) motivated God to allow this to happen. He knew that only JESUS possessed what it would take to redeem mankind back into fellowship with Him. Jesus was the only one who ever lead a totally sinless life. Therefore, He was the only one whose shed blood could pay for the sin debt of the whole world.

The Word of God says "The wages of sin is death; but the gift of God is eternal life through Christ our Lord" (Romans 6:23).

God gave His most precious possession (His Son JESUS) to die in our place, because we mean that much to God. He loves us with such a completely selfless, unconditional Love! Jesus was the only hope for mankind then and He still is today.

<u>JESUS GOD'S SON</u>: Even knowing the cruelty of the Cross, the shame and humiliation of it, and the false accusations that He would have to endure, JESUS still CHOSE to willingly be the sacrifice for us. Even knowing the time He would have to spend in Hell itself, did not change His mind. He would not be deterred from accomplishing what God sent Him to do. He loves God and us that much!

Jesus knew the mental, physical and emotional agony He would have to endure before and during His death on the Cross.

Out of sheer LOVE for us and God – and His desire to please His Heavenly Father, Jesus paid the ultimate price with His blood and His very life.

Jesus was willing to suffer, even to the awful moment in time when God had to turn His face from Him. Jesus became sin itself as He took upon Himself the sins of all mankind for all generations to come.

Jesus literally went to Hell for three days in order to atone for our sins.

WHY did He do that? The answer is the same once again – because of the LOVE Jesus has in His heart for each of us. Jesus knew, too, that He was mankind's only Hope. That has not changed.

Jesus' Love for us continues to be manifested even in Heaven today.

When we sin, "...Jesus Christ the righteous..." is our advocate before God The Father (I John 2:1).

Jesus said in Joh11:25 (kjv):

"I AM The Resurrection and the life; he [or she] that believeth in Me, though he[or she] were dead, yet shall he [or she] live."

THE HOLY SPIRIT OF GOD, (THE COMFORTER): The Holy Spirit is manifestation of The Living Jesus in the world today. He came when Jesus went back to Heaven. He IS the power to live the Christian life today. He, too, loves us very much.

At the time of your Salvation, when God the Father was drawing you to Himself, it was The Holy Spirit who was reaching inside your heart and tugging at it. He was convicting you of your sins, making good changes in your heart and bringing you to the point of repentance. The Holy Spirit empowers and helps you change as you become conformed to the image of Christ Jesus, as was predestined by God (Romans 8:29a). The Holy Spirit does that same thing with all Christians.

The Holy Spirit makes intercession for you all the time "...according to the will of God" (Rom. 8:27). He is at work every day convicting you of sin, wrong thinking, attitudes or actions and, at the same time, encouraging you out of them!

It is through the power of The Holy Spirit that you communicate and have fellowship with God.

The Holy Spirit is that still small voice of God speaking to you today saying "...This is the way, walk ye in it..." (Isaiah 30:21).

He is your Comforter, walking along side of you, no matter what you're going through. He daily proves His Love by manifesting His presence in your life. He is forever leading and guiding you.

How then, do you return such LOVE to God, Jesus and The Holy Spirit?

First of all, you return it by allowing God, through the power of His Holy Spirit, to show you how much you are loved by each person of the Trinity.

Second, you return it by accepting, believing and praising God for that Love.

Third, you return it by being grateful and saying thank you to each person of the Trinity.

God wants you to know what your salvation costs each of them. But He also wants you to know that, in His eyes, YOU were, and are, worth the price!

Each one of us is very loved, wanted and valued in God's sight. That should definitely make you know, beyond a shadow of a doubt, that you are treasured by God.

Chapter Eleven

LEARNING TO TRUST GOD

How do you learn to trust someone? I mean really trust them. At what point are you confident enough in, and comfortable enough with, the other person to be willing to drop your guard and open up to them? At what point do you decide that it's okay to be completely and totally honest, open and transparent with the other person? At what point do you feel that you can trust the other person with the private, personal and important things of your life and heart?

What happens that causes you to know that regardless of what you say or do the other person's feelings toward, and acceptance of, you will not change, no matter what?

When do you know for sure that the other person would never intentionally do, or say, anything to hurt you?

How do you reach a point of knowing that the other person will always have your best interest at heart, regardless of the situation? What causes you to be confident, assured and at Peace about all these things?

How do you reach the point of being comfortable with someone spirit-to-spirit and soul-to-soul? At what point in the relationship or friendship does it happen? How and when does this happen? These are important questions.

THE ANSWER is simple. It happens over time. It happens when you spend time with the other person getting to know them, being around them, and observing them (what they do and say) in different situations and circumstances. Those different situations and circumstances will afford you many opportunities to see inside the heart, mind and soul of that person.

Trust happens when you see that they are consistent in their ethics, character, values, morals and temperament.

Trust happens when you hear in their words, and more importantly, see in their actions, that they are who they say they are at all times. This means there is consistency in who they are, regardless of whether anyone else is around or not.

Trust happens when you can see for yourself that the other person is genuine, that they can be trusted and that they honestly care about you (with no hidden agendas). It happens when someone has proven to you again and again that they are worthy of you putting your trust in them.

That's also how you learn
to
TRUST GOD!

Once God has shown you that He is the real deal, you will know, without reservation or hesitation that you can trust Him with everything in your life.

One of the things that testifies of God is referenced in John 5:39 where He says for us to "Search the Scriptures...they are they which testify of Me."

In order to trust God, you need to realize that Faith in God is not a feeling. It is "...simply taking GOD at His Word" (Campus Crusade for Christ).5

Please get into the habit of living in the knowledge that God will always stay true to Scripture (His Word), regardless of people, circumstances, anyone's feelings, desires or agendas, even yours.

You can totally trust that God does not lie. Numbers 23:19 says "God is not a man, that he should lie..." He will never violate His Word – ever!

Somewhere I heard someone say, "Faith is simply walking out what is already a fact in the eyes of God" (author unknown).

When you think about it, God made everything, knows everything and (Praise God) He controls everything. More good news is that He's crazy about His children!

He knows exactly what it will take to manifest His very best for you in all situations and circumstances. He already knows what decisions you will make and what you will and will not do. He knows your good points and your shortcomings (just as He does with all of us).

But, God still loves you totally, completely and unconditionally. He sees your potential use in The Kingdom of God even as a "New" Christian.

Time and distances are not factors in God's world. He sees the world from beginning to end, all at one time and at a single glance. He knows what each one of us is going to do (today, tomorrow and forever). He also knows the decisions we're going to make even before we make them, be they good or not-so-good. He knows just where to place each of us and when, so that He, through us, can accomplish His perfect will in our lives and those around us.

God has ALL the answers to all of life's problems now and forever! He's very willing to share that information with you if you will but ask.

His Word says "If any of you lacks wisdom, let him ask of God ...and it shall be given him" (James 1:5). God may not give you all of the answers you want right when you want them.

He will, however, give you the answers that you need when you need them. If it's not His time for something, He may just give you the grace to wait. He may also tell you to trust Him and step out in faith. Either way, whatever He says will be for your good. Never doubt that!

These are some of the essentials of the Christian life:

- Believing in Salvation through Jesus,
- Repenting and turning from your sins,
- Learning and Trusting in God's Word,
- Trusting God to honor His Word,
- Calling on, and being depend on, The Holy Spirit for help, guidance and direction, and
- Having a personal, and growing, relationship with God, Jesus and The Holy Spirit.

Philippians 4:19 says: "But my God shall supply all your need according to His riches in Glory by Christ Jesus." God, s we discussed earlier, is responsible for looking after your total basic needs, welfare, etc. That involves another form of trusting Him.

God does, however, expect us to do our part. For example, He expects us to tithe, buy food, clothing, and pay our bills, etc. with the funds that He's provides for us through our job or whatever means He gives the funds. He expects us to take care of our health and not abuse our bodies because we are the temple of The Holy Ghost (Spirit).

God is concerned about everything in your life, no matter what it might be. You will find that God cares about everything that pertains to you. If it's important to you, then it's important to Him.

When you allow God to prove His sovereignty, omnipotence and love for you, it becomes very easy to love and trust Him completely!

Walking humbly and staying close to Jesus is the key to success in this. Trusting Him and taking Him at His word just comes naturally once you get to know Him.

It's always good to keep a humble and teachable spirit before The Lord. Ask Him to give you a hunger and thirst for Him and the truth of His Word.

You will find that God is THE only source for everything you will ever need in this life and in the one to come.

Praise The Name of our Wonderful Lord Jesus!

- - - - - - - -

Chapter Twelve

LETTING GOD LOVE YOU

Loving, trusting and allowing someone (even GOD) to love you are all intertwined parts of the same thing. It may sound simple; but, it's not for some people.

Some folks are loners (some, by choice and some because they have never felt that they fit in). Many have felt this way most of their lives. They've bought into the lie of the devil (or someone else) who told them (or implied to them) that they are somehow not worthy, not good as, not good enough, or in some other way, inferior to everyone else. Many, though certainly not all, may never have felt loved and accepted by others. These people have not known much of having genuine love truly expressed to them by others. With some, this may go back many years - even to when they were a child.

Jesus, however, said of the little children "...for of such is the Kingdom of Heaven" (Matthew 19:14). In Mark 10:14 and Luke 18:16 it says "for of such is the kingdom of God."

For these folks, allowing God or people to love them is a new and sometimes awkward experience. It's much like an Eskimo's first trip to Florida. They just aren't sure initially whether, or not, they trust the new situation in which they find themselves, nor are they sure of the best way to respond (or even if they want to respond).

It's not that they do not want to love and be loved, far from it. However, most of what they have known all of their lives has been pain, hurt and rejection. They are accustomed to mattering very little, if at all, to other people. They've learned to live with little or no love in their lives. They don't strive with it any more. They have just accepted it. They are not on a Pity-Party. It's just the way life is for them in their way of thinking, at least up to this point in time.

For some, before JESUS became Lord of their lives, loneliness and reality were so painful that many of them withdrew into themselves. This inward retreat was a desperate attempt at self-preservation It was in the safety of their retreat (into themselves) that they were free from pain and hurt. They were not lonely because they had learned to be alone, even when in a crowd. I said all that to say this!

How then, do you, having lived this way for many years come to the place of letting The King of the Universe, The Lord God Almighty, The One who is love itself prove to you His awesome love for you?

THE ANSWER: By allowing God's Holy Spirit to change your heart and give you a new heart (I Samuel 10:9 and Ezekiel 11:19). May God give you a heart that responds to Him and His overflowing Agape Love for you – in Jesus' Name.

If you are one of the ones coming from this type of background, please know (regardless of what you have experienced in the past) that YOU are worth loving and are dearly loved and valued by God Almighty Himself! Know and be assured that God does not lie. He is worthy of your trust and you can believe what He says (including what He says about His love for you).

By God's Grace and in His Mercy, He will bring you to a point that you will be able to accept His love for you, if you haven't already!

It's definitely a whole lot easier to love and trust a perfect, Holy God, than to trust imperfect people who might possibly hurt you again. But don't be concerned, God is Faithful! He will bring you to a point of trusting Him even in relationships with others (maybe even with some of those who have hurt or rejected you). He will do this if you are willing to allow Him to work in your heart and make some changes in the way you see yourself and others, for everybody's good.

Allowing God to love you must begin by allowing Him to show you just how special You are to Him. He created you in your mother's womb even before you were born (Psalm 139:13-17). Why did He do that?

God wanted YOU! He has a plan and a purpose for you (Jeremiah 29:11). It's His plan and purpose for you to fulfill.

Take a minute right now and talk to God. Purpose [determine] in your heart to seek God with all your heart, mind and soul. Along with that ask Him to reveal His perfect will, plan, direction and calling for you.

Side note here please: You CANNOT seek the calling, etc. It is critical that you seek GOD. Then, when you're ready, He will reveal His calling to you.

Make the decision that, by His Grace, you will allow Him to accomplish His plan and purpose in and through you. That way when you stand before God, He will be able to say "...Well done, thou good and faithful servant" (Matthew 25:23) Remember, God chose the plan and purpose for you. It's perfect for you alone, because God makes no mistakes.

God's Love for you (and all of us) was proven to its fullest when Jesus died on the Cross in our place, was raised from the dead and ascended back to Heaven to be with God His Father. That was, and is, "The" greatest act of Love ever known to mankind. There will never be one greater!

Allowing Jesus to be your Savior and Lord in your life is only the first step (of many) in letting God love you.

God will prove His Love for you over and over in many different ways. Even in your weary places, God will show Himself strong and very present on your behalf. During those times He will find many ways to bless you, so many ways that some may even go unnoticed at first.

It's during those times, that some of your heart desires (you know, the ones you have not expressed to anyone) all of a sudden, may just happen or come to pass.

Romans 11:33 says "O the depth of the riches both of the wisdom and knowledge of God…and His ways past finding out." God does work in mysterious ways. He may choose to love you in simple ways (such as your favorite food unexpectedly being prepared for you). Or, He may work out circumstances so that now you have extra time for that much needed rest. Perhaps it will be that you now have more time for your family and friends. He may even increase your desire to spend more time studying His Word and talking with Him. Whatever way God chooses to manifest His love for you, you can be sure that He designed it just for you.

Another way of letting God love you is to allow Him to carry ALL of your burdens, (you know, the ones that you have been trying to carry and work out for yourself for such a long time now). Jesus said it very clearly, "Come unto Me, all you who are heavy laden and I will give you rest" (Matthew 11:28). He says "Take My yoke upon you and learn of Me; My yoke is easy and My burden is light" (Matthew 11:29).

God simply loves you! He never intended for you to carry any heavy burden by yourself. His shoulders are big and strong! It doesn't matter what's bothering you or trying to weigh you down, Jesus can handle it! Give all of your problems, worries, cares and concerns to Him! He can and will gladly handle them for you!

God uses times of special lovings and "Come unto Me and I will give you rest" (Matthew 11:28) as exactly that – times of mental, physical, spiritual and emotional rest! Learn to rest in Jesus! Let everything in your life (as best as you're able) flow forth from a place of being at peace and rest in Jesus.

These are times for just being still and leaning back in the strong arms of Jesus. He loves you in such a heart-felt way and to a depth that no human being ever can! None of us are capable of loving to that depth.

Finally, letting God love you is spending time with, drawing near to, and communing with Him. These times can be quiet times or times of praise. It really doesn't matter! It's all about being in each other's presence, just you and The Lord and delighting in each other's presence.

Let The Holy Spirit guide you as to what these times should be (and each one may be different). Whatever way He leads, these will be times of just resting in and knowing that God is God and that you're making His day by choosing to spend time with just Him. These are precious times of just relaxing and being at peace just enjoying Jesus!

An encouragement if I may - Know that God has everything under control and that nothing catches Him by surprise. He's got whatever is bothering you covered. Commit it to Him and leave it there! He can handle it! Receive God's Grace, Mercy and Love! It's wonderful!

GETTING STARTED! Some 1st Steps In Your Journey With Jesus!

Chapter Thirteen

WAITING ON THE LORD

Waiting on The Lord is not something that any of us like to do; and yet, God requires it of all of His children at some point in time!

No Christian walks very long with The Lord without experiencing this mountain of Spiritual growth. However, waiting on the Lord is definitely not the same thing as sitting and doing nothing!

If you are in one of those "Waiting on The Lord" times, just relax, be still and trust Him. Psalm 27:14 says, "Wait on The Lord...be of good courage...and He shall strengthen your heart..." God is working even now (behind the scenes) on your behalf in ways your natural eyes may not have seen yet. But, He's still working just the same!

Just as in a ballgame, the fact that a player is not out on the field every moment, does not mean that he is not still very much actively involved in the game.

So, just as in a ballgame, what should a player's response be when the coach says, "Sit this quarter out"?

First of all, there must be quick, total, and complete obedience! The player must trust the coach and quickly do exactly what the coach said, no more and no less.

Second, if that's you, look around you. Perhaps there are other players currently on the sidelines also. Get to know them (because, in reality, this is the Super Bowl of Eternal Life or lack thereof). Find out where the other people are in The Lord and what God is doing in their lives at this point in time. Encourage, teach and help them in whatever way you can during this time. Make yourself available for any way you can help them grow and develop, so they will be better equipped when they do go back on the playing field. Offer to Pray for them. Remember, if they are on God's Team, then you're both on the same team.

Join forces with them against discouragement, etc. Help them realize that it wasn't anything personal when the coach temporarily took them off the main playing field. His purpose and focus involves the welfare of everybody on the team, not just one person. You can never lose by helping, encouraging and lifting up someone else while both of you wait on The Lord to move.

God will always bless back to you whatever encouragement, etc. you give to another. As mentioned before, you can never out give God – in anything!

One more note, if God allows someone into your life during this time who does not yet know Him, use this time to tell them about Jesus and what He means to you (as The Holy Spirit leads and gives you opportunity). Or, it could be that God wants you to just pray for them. Either way, listen for The Holy Spirit to direct you in reference to what to say and pray and how to use your time.

Never fear! God can, and will, redeem whatever time you thought was lost while you were sitting and waiting on the sidelines.

Third, trust God that He knows what's best for you. It may be that you've been working too hard (really giving it your all). God loves you too much to allow you to continue doing that. In His Wisdom, it could be that He knows you need a rest. It could be that this time of Waiting on The Lord and resting was exactly what you needed to get you back on your feet, even much stronger than before.

Fourth, trust God to know exactly when to put you back into the more active part of the game. In reality, you were never really out of the game, just viewing it from a different place for a season.

Remember this:

God's timing is always perfect,

simply because

HE is!

- - - - - - - -

Chapter Fourteen

WHAT ABOUT TITHING?
Does it matter?

THE ANSWER: In a nutshell – "YES," very much so! Tithing is a foundational Bible principle for all of God's children.

God promises to provide the needs of His Children (Philippians 4:19). You notice I said "needs" not wants. Many times God will make known His will through funds provided, as well as times of funds withheld. The purpose of one is just as important as the other in what God is doing in your life and situation. This includes you and any others who are involved in the situation.

If the funds aren't there, the first thing to look at is the question "Are you tithing as the Scripture has said do?" If not, you need to get that corrected as soon as possible.

There's such a multitude of reasons of why God may be allowing things to happen as they are; but, you have to always start with the Tithe. If you're a tithing child of God, then God will somehow intervene; because He says in Scripture that He will supply your need.

Here are several possibilities as to why the funds aren't there when needed:

1. Maybe God has provided the funds and, for whatever reason, you've misspent them on wrong things, or in wrong ways. If that's the case, all you can do is repent, ask God's forgiveness and ask Him to redeem the error that you made. Ask Him, also, to grant you the Grace to not make the same mistake again. That's very important.

2. God might be trying to turn you in a different direction in some way.

3. Perhaps He's trying to teach you to learn to be more totally dependent on Him for your daily bread (so-to-speak), while at the same time, being at Peace that He has everything under control.

4. Perhaps He's leading you to seek out a different job, or maybe a different living situation.

5. Perhaps He's using your situation to show Himself strong on your behalf and also as

a testimony of proof of His presence to the watching world around you.

6. Perhaps God is using your situation to teach others to have more compassion on those who are struggling financially. Only God knows why He's allowing this, but He will tell you in His time.

One thing I do need to mention because, as a new Christian, you may not have even thought about it yet. That is, that since you gave your life to Jesus, He now has the right to use your situation in whatever way serves His purpose in your life and in the lives of others also.

So PRAY that ALL concerned will learn quickly whatever it is that The Lord wants each of you to learn, so you can get past the current situation as soon as possible.

Seek God diligently as to what is happening in your life about your finances.

Another way to experience true communication with God about finances (or anything else) is to look into His Word. Study and read Scripture for yourself. That way you will know whether, or not, that which you are asking God for lines up with The Word of God. If it doesn't, He is under no obligation to provide it for you.

For a Tithing Child of God, God promises "...to pour out a Blessing that there shall not be room enough to receive it" (Malachi 3:10). In that same Scripture, He invites you to prove Him in the area of the tithe.

A look at Scripture will also clear up a misunderstanding about the tithe that some Christians have. Some think they are doing right by giving part, or all, or their tithe money to help someone in need. And, Yes, certainly help someone in need if you can (that's definitely Bible), but not with your tithe money. That's not what Scripture tells us to do with the tithe.

The Bible says in Malachi 3:10, "...bring ye ALL the tithes into the storehouse..." Scripture is very clear about that. The storehouse is the church at which you're being Spiritually fed.

Before becoming a Christian you probably knew very little about tithing. The beginning of tithing goes all the way back to the Old Testament times. For example, the sheep had to pass under a counting stick. Every tenth one was the Lord's as the tithe, and it was Holy unto Him (Leviticus 27:31) Even if that tenth one was a perfect lamb (which meant it might have been used for breeding), that did not matter. Leviticus 27:31 says: "...if a man will at all redeem ought of his tithes, he shall add thereto the fifth part thereof." I've heard that explained that if a man argues with God about the tenth one, then God will require the fifth one after that. That in essence becomes twenty percent rather than the ten percent that God initially required.

The moral to the story is to cheerfully give back to God the ten percent (that belongs to Him anyway). Be grateful that He's allowing you to keep and use the other ninety percent and will bless it and make it go further.

The money is not the important thing to The Lord anyway. He wants your heart and your obedience to Scripture. The ten percent tithe brought into the storehouse (the church) is so that "...there will be meat in mine house..." (Malachi 3:10). When you surrender your all to The Lord and come to understand His ways, you will realize that ALL you have belongs to God anyway. That's when you will cheerfully, willingly and freely give the ten percent (and beyond) as The Holy Spirit leads you.

A Caution here please:

Don't fall for the lie of the devil when he tries to tell you that you cannot afford to tithe. Reality is that you can't afford not to tithe because God (in Scripture) has told you to tithe. Scripture tells of consequences if you argue with God about the tenth, He requires even more as mentioned above.

One of the greatest Blessings of tithing is that you know you have been obedient to God's Word. God said when you tithe that He will rebuke the devourer on your behalf (Malachi 3:11). You will find your money going much further and things lasting longer than you thought possible.

Give, Child of God, not because you have to, not out of obligation, but in obedience to God's Word. Give because you love Jesus and are grateful for all He has done for you. It's a privilege.

- - - - - - - -

Chapter Fifteen

SOME OLD TESTAMENT NAMES FOR GOD AND THEIR MEANINGS

ADONAI
> SOVEREIGN LORD.
> Genesis 15:2

ELOHIM
> CREATOR GOD, OMNIPOTENT.
> Genesis 1:2

EL ELYON
> SOVEREIGN.
> Genesis 14:18

EL-SHA-DDAI
> ALL SUFFICIENT ONE.
> Genesis 17:1

JEHOVAH   (YHWH)
> GOD OF REVELATION.
> Genesis 2:4

JEHOVAH-JIREH

PROVIDER.
Genesis 22:14

JEHOVAH-M'KADDESH (or Mekoddishkem),
GOD WHO SANCTIFIES.
Exodus 31:13

JEHOVAH-NISSI
A BANNER FOR HIS PEOPLE
Exodus 17:15

JEHOVAH-ROHI (Or Roeh)
SHEPHERD.
Psalm 23.

JEHOVAH-ROPHE – HEALER.
Exodus 15:26

JEHOVAH-SHALOM – PEACE.
Judges 6:24

JEHOVAH-SHAMMAH
GOD WHO IS PRESENT.
Ezekiel 48:35

JEHOVAH-TSIDKENU
OUR RIGHTEOUSNESS, Jeremiah 23:6

Learning these names and what they mean will help you get to know more about God and His character.

- - - - - - - -

GETTING STARTED! Some 1st Steps In Your Journey With Jesus!

Chapter Sixteen

MOVING FORWARD - VARIOUS WAYS TO STUDY *THE BIBLE*

1. PASSAGES	"Herein is Love…"
2. WORDS	"Covenant"
3. DOCTRINES	"Baptism"
4. THOUGHTS	"God is Everywhere"
5. NAMES	"Jehovah"
6. PEOPLE	"Mary"
7. BOOK BY BOOK	"Matthew, Mark, Luke, John, etc."

Dr. Ralph Richardson
(Used by permission 1994). 10

Getting back to reading and studying Scriptures, if you (as a New Christian) have absolutely no idea of where to start reading in Scripture, I recommend the book of John or even the book of Matthew.

The Old Testament is not necessarily the easiest place to begin reading on a regular basis; unless God impresses it upon your heart that (for whatever reason) He wants you to start reading there. If you feel led to begin reading there, certainly do so and God will honor your obedience.

If you in a Sunday School or Bible study read whatever they are studying.

If you aren't aware of any Bible study groups in your church, you might consider asking your pastor, your Sunday School teacher or even the pastor's Administrative Assistant if they know of any Bible studies currently being held or coming up soon.

Just make sure that whoever is teaching the Bible study believes in the inerrant, infallible truth of God's Word. That's important question to ask.

Another suggestion is that you start a routine of reading five Psalms a day and also one chapter of Proverbs a day.

There are 150 Psalms. Therefore, in a thirty-day month you will have read through the entire Book of Psalms. There are thirty-one chapters of

Proverbs. By reading one chapter a day (and doubling up on the last day), you will also have read through all of Proverbs in a month. I'm heard this method suggested several times over the years; so it is not original with me. I do not recall who it came from initially, but it's a good place to start. If you feel you can't, or don't have time, to read both Psalms and Proverbs each day, maybe just start with one chapter of Proverbs a day, plus whatever other reading God has prompted you to do.

Again, please pray and let The Holy Spirit guide you as to where to begin reading on a DAILY basis. If you commit your time to God in Prayer, The Holy Spirit will prompt you as to exactly where to read at that particular point in time. Simply be obedient to His leading.

Remember please to always PRAY FIRST and ask The Holy Spirit to reveal God, Jesus and the truth of God's Word to you as you read and study. It's important – and God will honor that.

- - - - - - -

GETTING STARTED! Some 1st Steps In Your Journey With Jesus!

Chapter Seventeen

WHICH VERSION OF THE BIBLE TO USE?

I have found *The Living Bible* to be a good place for New Christians to start. I'm not sure if it's still in print or not. It's a paraphrase of The Bible (not a translation) and was first published in 1971. Stay with the original on this if you buy it.

The Living Bible was written by Dr. Kenneth Taylor for his children (and/or grandchildren) best I remember. It was purposely written to be an easier to read and simpler form of Scripture.

If you can't find a copy, I recommend the NEW King James Version of *The Bible.*

I use the King James Version of *The Bible*, but it might not be the best one for a New Christian initially. A former Pastor of mine used the New American Standard Version of *The Bible*. Any of these are good.

You might start with whatever version of *The Bible* you currently have at home, and see how that goes. You can always switch to another version later.

You might also ask your pastor which version of *The Bible* he preaches from in the church services.

My prayer is that God will lead you to exactly the version of *The Bible* that He wants you to read and study. I pray this for you in the powerful Name of Jesus. Amen.

Remember, The Holy Spirit is the Teacher and The One who reveals truth and understanding, regardless of which version of *The Bible* you use. However, you would be wise to stay with a version that has proven to be true over the years. Your pastor should be able to help if you have questions.

Just as information – my understanding is that:

<u>A Translation</u> is a direct word for word from the original Hebrew, Aramaic, and Greek documents. The King James Bible is one of the translations.

<u>A Paraphrase</u> is a version of *The Bible* where the Author is putting it into their own words. *The Living Bible* is one of the paraphrased Bibles.

Again, The Holy Spirit is the teacher and the one who give revelation and insight into all Scripture regardless of the version.

Chapter Eighteen

SOME BASIC HELPLFUL TOOLS

1. BIBLE RESEARCH WEBSITES

Biblegateway.com. is one such website. In today's age of technology there are probably others also.

One Caution: If you use an on-line Bible search program, be careful to select which version of *The Bible* you want to read. Sometimes you have to re-select the version over and over to keep it showing.

Save the website as one of your favorites or bookmarks (with that version of *The Bible* showing) at the time when you actually save it. Sometimes that will hold the version of *The Bible* you selected. If it doesn't, just take a quick minute the next time you go back on-line and check it. If it needs to be changed, just switch it back to the correct version that you want to read and research whatever.

2. **A BIBLE DICTIONARY**

Unger's is one. Vines is another.
I'm sure there are others to choose from also. These may help you understand some definitions as a new Christian.

3. **A CONCORDANCE**

Strong's Concordance is a good one. However, unless you're planning to get into the Greek or Hebrew meanings of the words, you might want to wait on this book initially.

There are print versions. The one I have is a big book, two to three inches thick from many years ago. In today's electronic age, it's probably available on line, or in a downloadable version. Your church bookstore or a local Christian book store would know.

4. **A COMMENTARY**

I know that many people use commentaries, I do not. That's a decision you will need to pray about and led The Holy Spirit lead you. The Lord has always just led me to just stay with Scripture and let The Holy Spirit interpret it for me or let Scripture confirm itself in whatever way.

If you do choose to use a commentary, be careful about which one you use. I saw somewhere that the Preacher Charles Spurgeon, recommended a commentary by Matthew Henry many years ago. I think you can still get a copy. When in doubt, talk with your pastor, he may tell you to just stick with *The Bible* and let The Holy Spirit teach and guide you.

The most accurate and purest way to understand Scripture (that I have found) is to get into the habit of praying before you read and meditate on Scripture and ask God to bless and enlighten your understanding of it. Ask The Holy Spirit to reveal (illuminate) Scripture to you. Put the responsibility of your understanding of the Scripture back into the hands of The Holy Spirit.

But you do your part, by asking for His help, wisdom, guidance, discernment and understanding.

God will honor a prayer prayed from the heart of one who is seeking to know Him - and the truth of His Word.

Scripture should ALWAYS be the primary source of where you get your understanding of God, Jesus and The Holy Spirit.

The Word of God says it best:

"Study to show thyself approved unto God...rightly dividing the Word of Truth" (II Timothy 2:15).

- - - - - - - -

Chapter Nineteen

A DAILY QUIET TIME

What is a Daily Quiet Time? It's a time that you choose to set aside each day to just spend time alone with God and His Word.

It's a great time to study *The Bible*, talk with God about what's on your heart, and listen to Him about what's on His.

There are no hard and fast guidelines as to how you spend your Quiet Time with The Lord, except to Pray and ask God to bless your time together.

Daily Quiet Times can be as little as ten to fifteen minutes per day to several hours per day (if you have the time to give). The amount of time you commit to is between you and The Lord. The main thing is staying faithful and consistent to whatever amount of time you and The Lord agree upon. Sometimes things come up and you can't have your normal Quiet Time that day. God understands that. Don't beat yourself up about it if that happens. Grab ten or fifteen minutes somewhere else in the day (or evening) if you can.

If not, just get back on your regular Quiet Time schedule the next day. It's okay.

I would offer one caution. If you start missing a lot of daily Quiet Times, you would be wise to take what's happening back to The Lord and talk with Him about it. He will show you what, if any, changes need to be made on your part; but don't keep ignoring it if that's what's happening.

God knows your schedule and responsibilities (and everybody else's too). Seek Him about how much time to start off with in your commitment to this. If you need to, adjust the amount of time later.

So, how do you get started in a Quiet Time with The Lord? Actually Scripture tells us how to do it.

"Enter into His Gates with Thanksgiving, and into His Courts with Praise: Be Thankful unto Him and Bless His Name" (Psalm 100:4). This can be in the form of singing to God or just verbally praising Him. I don't think it matters to God which way you choose. He's just delighted that you've chosen to spend this time alone with Him. He loves time with you, simply because He loves you!

- - - - - - - -

A SUGGESTION (just to help get you started) –

Your Quiet Time might include these, starting with entering into His gates with Thanksgiving and into His courts with Praise:

1. A Time of Thanksgiving.
2. A Time of Praise.
3. A Time of Prayer.
4. Scripture Reading.
5. Scripture Meditation.
6. Talking to God.
7. Listening to God.
8. A Closing Prayer of Gratitude.

The main thing is to be open, sensitive and obedient to the leading of The Holy Spirit. He will lead you as to how God wants your time together to be used.

Allowing The Holy Spirit to lead in the flow of things is always the best way. It's where you'll experience the greatest blessing and receive the most benefit from your time with The Lord!

Enjoy those times! They are precious fellowship times with God, Jesus and The Holy Spirit!

- - - - - - - - -

GETTING STARTED! Some 1st Steps In Your Journey With Jesus!

Chapter Twenty

OTHER INSIGHTS FROM SCRIPTURE

The Word of God says "Trust in the Lord with all your heart; and lean not unto your own understanding. In all your ways to acknowledge Him, and He shall direct your paths" (Proverbs 3:5, 6).

God said, "For as the Heavens are higher than the Earth, so are my ways higher than your ways, and my thoughts than your thoughts" (Isaiah 55:9).

However, as one pastor said, "But God does not want it to be that way. He wants us to know Him and His ways and for them to be our thoughts and our ways also." (Byerly). [4]

Delight yourselves in the Lord and He will give you the desires of your heart is a beautiful promise (Psalm 37:4).

Delight yourself also that you serve a God whose ways and thoughts far exceed the geniuses of this world. There is great Comfort in knowing that He who knows it all – loves you! God is also committed to molding, melting, shaping and loving you (and all of His children) into the image of His

Son Jesus Christ. That's exciting, though not always pleasant, if we're resisting what He is trying to do.

It's important for you to know, that as a Child of God, you can expect God to answer you when you pray. Sometimes God says no, sometimes wait, sometimes He may tell you that it's not quite the right time or place yet. But, Praise God, many, many times, God says "Yes". His Word tells us in Psalm 84:11 that "...No good thing will He withhold from them who walk uprightly."

Psalm 62:5 says "My soul, wait thou only upon God; for my expectation is from Him."

Psalm 62:8 says "Trust in Him at all times; ye people, pour out your heart before Him, God is a refuge for us. Selah."

The Word of God says, "And this is the confidence that we have in Him, that, if we ask anything according to His will, He heareth us (I John 5:14)." Scripture goes on to say, "And if we know that He hear us, whatsoever we ask, we know that we have the petitions that we desired of Him" (I John 5:15).

If you have been a Christian very long, there's probably someone you're praying for to come to Salvation (to experience for themselves, the joy of knowing Jesus Christ as their own personal Savior). Rejoice! Good News! Every person's Salvation is definitely the will of God.

The Word of God says that He is "...not willing that any should perish but that all should come to repentance "(II Peter 3:9). However, God will not violate a person's free will (their right to choose) in order to get them there.

Have Faith in God! The Word of God says "...God hath dealt to every man [or woman] the measure of Faith" (Romans 12:3). That means that all of us have been given exactly the same amount of Faith. It also says "...without Faith, it is impossible to please Him [God]." How then is it possible that some people seem to have so much more Faith than others?

It's like when a baby is first born. The baby has absolutely every muscle he (or she) will ever need, even as an adult. However, the muscles develop (and become stronger) as the child grows and uses them

The same is true for us spiritually. The more we use our Faith, the stronger it becomes.

GETTING STARTED! Some 1st Steps In Your Journey With Jesus!

Chapter Twenty One

WARNINGS FROM SCRIPTURE

This next section on Warnings from Scripture is not meant, in any way, to scare you, but to help make you "aware" of the seriousness of a couple of things.

It is meant to help you understand the seriousness of lying (especially to The Holy Spirit). Blaspheming The Holy Ghost is addressed in Chapter 8 of this book.

In the story in Acts 5:1-11. Peter said "...thou hast not lied unto men, but unto God" (Act: 5:4b).

The irony of the story about Ananias and Sapphira is that there was no need for them to lie. They owned some property and could do with it as they pleased. However, they sold some land, decided to keep back a part of the price and conceived in their hearts to lie to The Holy Spirit about the price that they received for the land.

Peter confronted each one of them separately. Each of them lied and each of them died - instantly. God's Word gives strong warnings to those who choose to lie. The Word of God (in

John8:44) talks about satan being the father of lies and that the truth is not in him.

God's Word says, "A false witness shall not be unpunished and he [or she] that speaketh lies shall perish" (Proverbs 19:9). Exodus 20:16 also states the command of God about bearing false witness against our neighbor.

I would encourage you that if you have a problem with lying, to confess it to God right now. Repent of it and cry out to God to deliver you from it. Please don't try to side-step it, or deny it. Come free from it – in Jesus' Name! God will help you - if you ask Him to help you! He will show you how to answer things with truth without having to lie. But, again, you have to ask Him to help you with this – from a sincere heart and a true desire to stop the lying.

If you're guilty of lying, God knows it, and most everybody else knows it too. Don't waste your time in trying to justify the lying, even to yourself. If you do, you're only deceiving yourself. You're also deceiving yourself if you think that your lying doesn't hurt other people. Unfortunately, the ones who are most often hurt by the lies you tell are usually the ones you love the most and who are the closest to you. My guess is that you know this is true and you hate it, but lying, telling half-truths or distorting the fact for your good have become somewhat of a pattern for you. So, why then, not ask God to help you stop it? For your good (and everybody else's), please admit and deal with the truth of the matter, if you're guilty of these things; and you may not be. I hope you're not. But, if you are, please ask God to deliver you from feeling the need to lie - about anything. You may have been comfortable telling lies for many years. You may have gotten away with it previously; but I believe God is saying to you now, "No More!"

Somewhere along the way, I heard it said that some people lie because they think the truth will not get them what they want, or get them their way in whatever. People like that usually find some way to blame somebody else for whatever (or say that is was somebody else's idea) - no matter the situation. They seem to have great difficulty in taking responsibility for their own actions, words and thoughts.

Perhaps the real issue in this is about:

1. Wanting to have their own way in everything (which becomes self-centeredness manifested).
2. Wanting to look good to others (pride).
3. Wanting to be the "preferred" person.

4. Wanting to be in control of every situation (which becomes pride and insecurity manifested).
5. Or, all of the above. Only you and God know, but He does know - and He will help you - if you will ask Him - and let Him.

My understanding is that habitual liars and compulsive liars are people who have allowed themselves (for a long time on a regular basis) to constantly distort, twist, add to, or embellish the truth with lies or half-truths. Lying has become so second nature to them, that they're not even aware that they are doing it. They deceive themselves; because they actually believe the lies they tell themselves and other people.

Everything has become all about them and whatever they need to say (or do) to get the response or end result that they want.

They may have become so self-deceived (with their own lies) that if someone told them that they were lying, they would probably say, "No I'm not." This is because they are believing their own lies.

However, there is Hope! Lord willing, He will send someone who cares enough about them to confront them, with much love and humility, about what they are doing, and who will pray them through to deliverance from lying and into learning how to walk in truth. There is a great need for the person to come free from the self-deception of the lies and to walk and live in truth. Grant it, Heavenly Father - in the powerful Name of Jesus I pray.

If you're lying (for whatever reason), please ask God to give you the Grace to immediately stop. Ask Him to show you how to speak the truth in love (Ephesians 4:15) in whatever you say to anyone.

Another important thing is that when people realize that you lie, you lose creditability with them. They simply won't trust you anymore. You will have to prove to them over and over that you have repented and have stopped lying in order to earn back their trust. Even then, it may take a long time (maybe even years) before they will ever trust you again, if they do ever trust you again. Most people want others to trust them, so be worthy of their trust. God will help you, but you have to ask Him! Cry out to Him to help you with this! He will. Like with everything else in your life, God wants you walking in victory over sin. Jesus bought that for you.

The Word of God says:

> "And ye shall know the truth
> [JESUS is truth],
> and the truth shall set you free."
> (John 8:32)

I cry out, with you, for God to help you even now. I ask Him to have Mercy on you, to deliver and help you come free of all the lies and self-deception and to replace them with truth, His Truth, as only He can – in Jesus' Name.

The Word of God calls satan the accuser of the brethren (Revelation 12:10). When you tell lies and falsely accuse someone, just remember with whom you are dealing. Do you really want to be a part of anything satan is doing? I don't think so. If you're truly a Christian you want absolutely nothing to do with him, in even the smallest of ways.

> The Word of God says:
> "... all liars, shall have their part in the lake which burneth with fire and brimstone: which is the second death" (Rev. 21:8b).
>
> "For the fruit of the Spirit is in all goodness and righteous and truth". (Ephesians 5:9)

When you're looking for truth, you're really seeking Jesus, whether you realize it or not.

Jesus said, "I am the way, the truth, and the life…" (John 14:6a).

"But speaking the truth in Love..."
(Ephesians 4:15).

Jesus is YOUR answer!
The Word of God is YOUR answer!

Rejoice New Person in Christ!
There is Hope!

"...for with Christ all things are possible"
(Mark 10:27b).

II Corinthians 5:17 says, "Therefore if any man [or woman] be in Christ, he [or she] is a new creature: old things are passed away; behold all things are become new."

That's You!

By having accepted Jesus as Savior and Lord, you are "a new creature in Christ!"

Things may not always be easy, but, Praise God, you now have God, Jesus and The Holy Spirit walking every step of the way with you   God will help you, if you ask Him and are willing to be obedient to what He says through the leading of His Word and voice of The Holy Spirit.

My prayer is that you will do so quickly, in Jesus' Name, Amen.

- - - - - - - - -

Chapter Twenty Two

PRAYING FOR THE LOST

After much prayer, The Holy Spirit prompted me to add these last two chapters. One is on "Praying for The Lost" and the other is on "Talking with Someone about Salvation."

Since you are now a Child of God, these chapters should help you in knowing how to pray for the lost and also help you as you explain Salvation to someone else. Once you know the awesomeness of knowing Jesus personally, you can't help but want others to know the joy that comes from knowing Jesus as Savior and Lord.

Don't feel any pressure about telling others about Jesus at this time. God knows your heart and any reservations or feelings of inadequacy that you may have. He will help you have the confidence to talk with others about Him when the time is right. But do start praying for the lost now. What He wants from you initially is for you to allow yourself to be discipled by His Word and get to know Him and Jesus on a more personal basis by the power, presence and anointing of The Holy Spirit.

So, read the information in these two chapters and refer back to them as needed, because they are here to help you as The Lord leads.

I trust that The Holy Spirit will anoint these writings, bless your understanding and prepare the hearts of all the lost, so that God can bring them to Salvation through faith in our Lord and Savior Jesus Christ.

- - - - - - - -

Chapter Twenty Three

SOME SCRIPTURES TO PRAY WHEN PRAYING FOR THE LOST

Here are some Scriptures that The Lord gave me in reference to "Praying for The Lost" (any who do not yet know Jesus Christ as Savior and Lord).

Blessings to you as you pray the Scriptures for whomever God lays on your heart - in Jesus' Name. May He give Spiritual fruit for your labor – in Jesus' Name, Amen.

PRAY – Thank God for whomever's salvation (name the person you are praying for) and commit the entire situation to God. Resist the devil on their behalf and tell him to flee (to take his hands off of them and their life and circumstances). This, however, really needs to be done by them. But you can agree with them in prayer about it. Ask God to replace where the evil was in their lives with an awareness of The Holy Spirit and the things of God's Word. As soon as they are saved, encourage the person to do what James 4:7 tells the Christian to do - and to do it as often as it's needed.

PRAY – Thank God that it is not His will that any should perish (2 Peter 3:9).

PRAY – Thank God that His Word says that anything we ask in His Name that He will give it (John 16:23-24).

PRAY – Thank God His Word says when any two agree as touching anything that it shall be done. (Matthew 18:19). Get together with another Christian and pray for this person's Salvation.

PRAY – Thank God that He will finish that which He starts and that Salvation is of Him (Psalm 68:19, 20).

In John 6:37 Jesus said:
"All that The Father GIVETH Me shall come to Me, and him [or her] that cometh to Me I will in no wise cast out." It doesn't matter what they've done, God will forgive their sins IF they genuinely repent and ask Him to forgive them. Praise God!

PRAY – Ask God to "GIVE" whomever you're praying for to Jesus – (based on the Scripture mentioned above). Name the person or people and any others who are lost. Ask that they be willing to "come" to Jesus, Who will, in no wise, cast them out, no matter what they've done - if they come with a repentant heart.

In John 6:40 Jesus said:
  "And THIS is the will of Him that sent Me, that everyone which seeth The Son, and Believeth on Him, may have everlasting life; and I will raise him [or her] up at the last day."

PRAY – Ask God to cause (Name the person or people) – to "SEE" Jesus (The Son of God) and "BELIEVE" on Him, that He is who Scripture says.

In John 6:44 Jesus said,
  "No man [or woman or child] can come to ME (Jesus), Except that The FATHER which hath sent Me draw him [or her]; and I will raise him [or her] up at the last day."

PRAY – Ask God, The Father in Heaven, to "DRAW" (Name the person or people) and anyone else who needs Salvation.

Romans 11:7 says:

"What then? Israel hath not obtained that which he seeketh for; but the election hath obtained it, and the rest were blinded."

PRAY – Ask God to cause all the lost to seek for Jesus and that they would not be blinded to "The One" they are seeking.

2 Corinthians 3:14 says:

"But their minds were blinded: for until this day remaineth the same vail untaken away in the reading of the Old Testament; which veil is done away in Christ."

2 Corinthians 4:4 says:

> "In whom the god of this world hath blinded the minds of them which believe not, lest the light of the glorious gospel of Christ, who is the image of God, should shine unto them."

PRAY – Ask God that the non-believers will be freed from the blindness of their minds.

PRAY that the Gospel of Christ will shine and be revealed to them.

1 John 2:11 says:

"But he that hateth his brother is in darkness, and walketh in darkness, and knoweth not whither he goeth, because that darkness hath blinded his eyes."

PRAY – Ask God to remove the darkness that has blinded the eyes of anyone who hates his [or her] brother [or sister]. Ask God to shine the light of His Word on their path so they can know where they are going and choose the right way – God's way.

OTHER MISCELLANEOUS THINGS TO PRAY:

Ask God to REVERSE what the enemy has done in the life of whomever. Ask Him to free the lost souls and gain back any ground that has been taken, or given over to the enemy. Ask Him to bring them to a saving knowledge of Jesus - in the powerful Name of Jesus.

PRAY – Ask God to remove anything and everything that is a hindrance to (Name the person you are praying for) coming to a saving knowledge of Jesus Christ (Isaiah 57:14).

PRAY – Ask God to remove any bad or wrong influences in this person's life and to replace them with Godly people.

PRAY – Ask God to give this person a spirit of humility and to not allow pride, a poor self-image, wrong prior teachings or wounded spirits to keep them from crying out to God for Salvation. PRAY in the Powerful Name of Jesus (Colossians 3:17).

PRAY – Thank God for the power of Prayer and for allowing you the privilege of lifting this person up to Him for Salvation.

Prayer (us being able to talk with God) is definitely both a privilege and a responsibility. What a wonderful gift God has given us - to be able to talk to Him and have Him speak to us about whomever.

Let the person you're praying for know that you are praying for them. It will be an encouragement to them (or should be anyway).

Child of God, take the time to thank God, even now, for hearing and answering the prayers you have lifted to him! It's important.

He loves
to hear gratefulness
from His children!

- - - - - - -

GETTING STARTED! Some 1st Steps In Your Journey With Jesus!

Chapter Twenty Four

TELLING OTHERS
ABOUT SALVATION
THROUGH JESUS CHRIST

When talking to a person about Salvation, consider something like this:

Salvation will only happen when you ask God to forgive your sins, call upon The name of The Lord Jesus, invite Jesus to come into your heart and life and believe on Him and that God has raised Him from the dead (Romans 10: 9,10,13).

It's important that you understand what Salvation is all about.

It's "THE" most important decision you will ever make in your entire life! The second most important decision you will ever make in your life is who you choose to marry, because that too affects your life, (and the lives of others), in a very big way for many years to come. So definitely pray about that one too.

However, without question, SALVATION is absolutely the most important decision of your life! It determines where you will spend eternity and who you will spend it with – Jesus and other fellow

Christians – or satan and his angels and those who have rejected Christ and what He did through His shed blood on Calvary.

Sometimes, people have questions or doubts about their Salvation (for a multitude of reasons). It this is you, and you think you're a Christian, but you're not sure, it's important that you go right away and talk with your pastor (or some other mature Christian who has been walking with Jesus for a long time). Ask them to pray with you and ask God to reveal anything that's causing the doubts and to show you how to come free from them.

If you have doubts about your Salvation that won't go away, then call upon The Name of The Lord "again".

Settle the genuineness of your Salvation in your heart and spirit! Pray again, the Prayer of Salvation (if you need to do that). Then document the date. If the devil ever tries to get you to doubt your Salvation again, you can just refer back to that date as a definite day and place that you accepted Jesus as Savior. This idea is not original with me, but it's a great idea. One more note, be sure to tell someone what you've done and when you did it.

You probably don't have any doubts about your Salvation, but just in case you do (even the slightest ones) just know that you don't have to live with any doubts at all, or buy into satan's lies that you are not saved.

You need to remember that Scripture says that satan is a liar (John 8:44).

Look a little further, if needed. One of the things that might cause you to doubt your Salvation is any sin in your life that has not been confessed, repented of and asked forgiveness for yet. If that's the case, simply deal with it. Make it right with God (and anyone else it needs to be addressed with, at least as much as is possible on your part).

It's important that you also know that *The Bible* (The Word of God) says that you can know that you are a child of God. Romans 8:16 says" "The Spirit itself beareth witness with our spirit, that we ARE the children of God." God does not want you living with doubts about this.

The Word of God says in Romans 10:9-10 that if you confess with your mouth The Lord Jesus and believe in your heart that God raised Him from the dead, that you WILL be saved. For it's with the heart man [woman or child] believes unto righteousness and with the mouth confession IS made unto Salvation.

Romans 10:13 goes on to say, "For whosoever shall call upon The Name of The Lord SHALL be saved."

Note that it says "shall be" saved -
(not might be) saved!

The Word of God says, "Herein is Love, not that we loved God, but that HE (God) loved us and sent His Son to be the propitiation [Atoning Sacrifice] for our sins" (I John 4:10).

John 3:16 says, "For God so loved the world that He gave His only begotten Son that whosoever believeth in Him should NOT perish, but have everlasting life."

Salvation is accepting what JESUS did on Calvary - (His death and His shed blood that paid the sin debt for ALL of man-kind) and His resurrection from the dead on the third day.

Salvation not only reveals the depth of God's love for us (and Jesus' too), but accepting it gives us the assurance that we will go to Heaven when we die. Thank You Heavenly Father! Thank You Jesus! Thank You Holy Spirit!

HOW POWERFUL AND LIFE-CHANGING THAT IS -
(both here and now - and in eternity)!

As great as things like giving to the poor and being a good moral person are, they will not get you into Heaven. They are good things, but JESUS, in

The Word of God said, "...I am the way, the truth and the life: no man [woman or child] cometh unto The Father, but by Me" (John 14:6).

It has to be through the shed blood of Jesus that a person comes to God. Scripture says, "...and without the shedding of blood, is no remission" (Hebrews 9:22).

Do yourself a favor, at the same time that you ask Jesus to be your SAVIOR, go ahead and ask Him to be Lord of your life.

It makes a world of difference when you allow JESUS to be the Lord of your life! By doing that, you are acknowledging that He knows so more than you in all things (and you want Him to be in control of everything in your life)!

Unfortunately, there may even be some who are reading this book who have never actually asked Jesus to come into their heart, forgive their sins and save their soul. They've thought about it and considered it many times, but have never actually gotten around to asking Jesus into their heart and life.

You know if that person is you. More importantly, God knows if that person is you. You may be able to fool some people. You may even be able to fool yourself into believing something that you know is not true; but you can't fool God. He knows the truth, and so do you.

My fervent prayer (James 5:16) is that IF that person is YOU, that you will stop reading right now (no time like the present). Take a minute, bow your head and genuinely pray the sinner's prayer of repentance unto Salvation. Ask Jesus to come into your heart and life.

Perhaps this illustration will help you understand Salvation. Suppose someone has a gift for you, one more valuable than you could ever have imagined.

Even though the gift is yours and is there waiting for you, it can never actually be yours, (and you won't be able to enjoy and appreciate it) until you actually accept the gift from the other person.

That's the way it is with the Gift of Salvation that God has for you. You cannot enjoy the benefits of being a Christian until they are one. So, please take the time to make sure that you are one.

Then go and tell somebody that you accepted Jesus as your Savior! It's very important that you do this because (as mentioned before) it's with the heart that you "believe unto righteousness" and "with the mouth confession is made unto Salvation" (Romans 10:10).

Then follow through and be baptized as stated in Acts 2:38 "...repent and be baptized every one of you in The Name of Jesus Christ." Jesus knew the need to be baptized and He was. Follow His example and the command of Scripture.

If you are a Christian, and have peace in your heart and spirit that you are, my suggestion is that you take a minute, pray and thank God for your Salvation.

One of your most powerful Spiritual weapons IS, and always will be - PRAYER! You will be wise to make Prayer a daily habit. In fact, pray often (at all times of the day and night) as The Holy Spirit leads.

"...Ask and ye shall receive, that your Joy may be full." (John 16:24).

Sharing what Jesus has done in your life and how you came to Salvation through Him is one of the most effective ways to tell others about Salvation – as The Holy Spirit leads.

- - - - - - - - -

GETTING STARTED! Some 1st Steps In Your Journey With Jesus!

Dear Reader,

Thank you for taking the time to read this book. I pray The Holy Spirit has revealed God, Jesus and Himself (or more about them) to you.

Please pray that God will use this book to feed His lambs and sheep and help them all come into a deep, personal relationship with God, our Heavenly Father, Jesus, our Savior and Lord and The Holy Spirit.

Praise God for The Holy Spirit who empowers and lives the Christian life in and through us. What a precious Gift our Heavenly Father has given us. My fervent prayer for you is that God will fill each of you to overflowing with love for Him, Jesus and God's Word (*The Bible*). May He open your eyes and allow each of you to see just how much He loves you and how precious you are in His sight. May He reveal His perfect will and plan for your life and give you the Grace to fulfill it for your good and His Glory! It's in the most beautiful, wonderful, powerful and majestic Name of our Lord Jesus Christ that I pray these things and thank Him for the reality of them.

Amen and Amen.

THANK YOU HEAVENLY FATHER, LORD JESUS AND HOLY SPIRIT!

May everything in this book be used for Your Purposes and Glory. I ask that all who read, hear, or hear about, this book come to know and love You as I do. Grant that this book will help them tremendously in their walk with You (especially the new and young Christians).

Heavenly Father only YOU can make this Prayer request a reality. Glorify Yourself, make Your power and presence known. All these things I ask in The Holy Name of Jesus Christ, my Savior, Lord and friend! Amen.

Thank You for allowing me the privilege of helping to feed Your lambs and Your sheep (John 21:15-17) through the writing of this book. I am very grateful. I love You Heavenly Father, Jesus and Holy Spirit.

Handmaiden4Him
Mary C. Brooks

GETTING STARTED! Some 1ˢᵗ Steps In Your Journey With Jesus!

BIBLIOGRAPHY

1. All Scriptures from the King James Version of *The Bible*. Nashville, Tenn. Thomas Nelson Publishers. 1989.

2. All Dictionary Definitions from <u>Webster's Ninth New Collegiate Dictionary</u>. Springfield, Mass. Merriam-Webster Inc. Pub. 1985.

3. BACK TO *THE BIBLE* RADIO BROADCAST. (Date Unknown).

4. BYERLY, Rev. Allan. Rocky Mt., NC.

5. *FAITH IS NOT A FEELING*. Campus Crusade for Christ. California.

6. HALL, Rev. Jim Charlotte, NC.

7. LORD, Rev. Peter. CBU Conference Black Mountain, NC. 1981.

8. RICHARDSON, Dr. Ralph. President Carolina Bible College. Fayetteville, NC.

BIBLIOGRAPHY (Continued)

9. SHELDON, Charles. *In His Steps*.
   Springdale, PA. Whitaker House. 1979.

10. STANLEY, Dr. Charles.
    In Touch Ministries.
    Atlanta, GA.

Used by Permission:
   The Voice of God,
      Rev. Peter Lord (1994).
   Ways to Study *The Bible*,
      Dr. Ralph Richardson (1994).

GETTING STARTED! Some 1st Steps In Your Journey With Jesus!

www.ingramcontent.com/pod-product-compliance
Lightning Source LLC
Chambersburg PA
CBHW061644040426
42446CB00010B/1578